YOU SEE **A HERO**, I SEE A
HUMAN BEING

DAVID A. ROBINSON, ESQ.

Momentum Books L.L.C.
Troy, Michigan

Printed and bound in the U.S.A.
Published by Momentum Books, L.L.C.
5750 New King Drive, Ste. 100
Troy, Michigan 48098
www.momentumbooks.com

Cover photo by Martin Vecchio.

ISBN-13: 978-1-938018-12-1
LCCN: 2019903813

This book is dedicated to my mother, Estella Marie Robinson, who inspired me at a young age to fight for what's right.

I also dedicate this book to all those I have represented, especially the many clients whose cases I cannot talk about because of confidentiality agreements.

This book is also dedicated to the white TACT officer who told me at our academy graduation, "We will never be equal." He was so right.

David A. Robinson was selected to recite the Law Enforcement Code of Ethics at his police academy graduation in 1975. All graduates were required to memorize the code, with the recruit who could deliver it best being chosen to present it at the ceremony. That honor went to Robinson, who continues to believe strongly that doing the right thing and treating all human beings with the dignity that they deserve are basic tenets of police work — and life.

OPENING STATEMENT

The job of being a police officer can be scary, unpredictable, rewarding, thankless, psychologically and emotionally challenging and, of course, deadly. It requires a special person to handle all that is necessary to fulfill the role society calls "police officer."

In the 100-plus years since the origin of policing in the United States, these characteristics of policing have remained constant. Behind every corner can lurk danger and excitement. Every call can be the last.

But in the past 41 years, the tools designed to assist police officers have improved dramatically. Today, they have access to Tasers (which are called "non-lethal" alternatives to deadly force); in-car video; traffic cameras; private businesses with cameras; body microphones; compliance tactics; training regimens; weapons; information accessibility; and other advancements.

These innovations, along with vastly improved communication between scout car and dispatcher and pressure point control tactics, are designed to minimize the use of force on citizens and to protect officers.

One result of these new tools is that the public can witness in a new way the mind and mentality of police officers — how they manage, and sometimes mismanage, the role and duties of policing. This is a game changer — and, for the most part, a good one. So it might be logical to conclude that all is well in police work.

But all is not well, as we so often see in the daily news. That's because the human factor, not tools, controls and dictates each citizen-police encounter. This human factor is a common denominator of man. It never has changed, and it never will.

To this end, it's crucial to keep in mind:

- A cop who was a thug before becoming a cop will still be a thug when engaging.
- A cop who stole before becoming a cop will have trouble resisting temptations to steal.
- A cop who had sexual perversions before becoming a cop, by the very nature of the job, can have his appetite readily quenched, unless he finds a way to deflect this propensity.
- A cop who was scared before becoming a cop can take a life wrongfully — and then effortlessly lie about it.

Conversely, a cop of strong character largely free of such flaws is far better able to enforce the law equitably and fairly and face the non-stop demands of his or her job.

The point is that the inherent danger of the role of police officer cannot and should not serve as the excuse for any form of misconduct. When officers try to rationalize misconduct, police chiefs, judges, juries, prosecutors and citizens must call it out. Only then can the process of policing work for the participants in the dichotomy of policing. And yet, all too often, this is not occurring.

Many prosecutors and judges know that holding cops accountable can ruin careers, and they think that's too high a price to pay, given their service. So prosecutors and judges operate with due deference — by not second-guessing the cop.

For instance, the grand jury testimony transcript in the now-infamous Ferguson, Mo., case of Michael Brown, who was shot to death by Officer Darren Wilson, reads like a Hollywood script. In what was a self-serving, one-sided version of events, the prosecutor simply let Wilson tell his story. "So, what happened next?" was her most common question. The process was calculated to result in no indictment. Failing to hold police accountable disserves officers, offends citizens and, as we have seen, invokes them to react to unjustified situations — and the officers involved in them. Thus, covering up or rationalizing misconduct by authorities who judge police behavior through "blue spectacles" actually reduces police officer safety.

The ideal police officers — and there are many — instinctively, and also consciously, employ their own human attributes of compassion, intelligence and patience to balance the challenges of their role to coexist with the rights of citizens they serve.

This book is inspired by the rash of police shooting incidents that have become public mainly because cameras are everywhere — and they do not lie. Along with the cases in my home state of Michigan that I describe in this book, the list of citizens besides Michael Brown across the country who have found themselves facing cops whose personality traits are ill-fitted for the job is long: Tamar Rice in Cleveland, Ohio; Eric Garner in Staten Island, New York City, N.Y.; Philando Castile in Falcon Heights, near St. Paul, Minn.; Alton Sterling in Baton Rouge, La.; Laquan McDonald in Chicago; Eric Harris in Tulsa, Okla.; Walter Scott in North Charleston, S.C.; Freddie Gray in Baltimore, Md.; Sandra Bland in Waller County, Texas; and Terence Crutcher in Tulsa, Okla., among them.

Sadly, this list of incidents is woefully incomplete. Where video evidence does not exist, the preeminence of the cops' words over those of citizens prevails. The misconduct may never be exposed.

Staunch police advocates will argue these cases should not be second-guessed, and that in each case, the officer was justified in using deadly force. As a former police officer, I see the dangerous flaw in this thinking; it is dangerous not only to the citizen, but also to the police officer.

I will explain why by a thorough analysis of the long-entrenched culture that pervades police work, and the institutions and people who, often unknowingly, enable that culture to thrive unchecked.

In this book, I will share my own lifelong experiences, observations of various cases and advice in "all-things-cops." I will offer my own story through the lens of my experiences as:

- An African American growing up in the 1960s and 1970s;
- An African American police officer for the Detroit Police Department in the 1970s and '80s;
- An attorney: Since leaving the DPD in 1988, I have remained deeply engaged in police culture through ongoing training, knowledge and firsthand experience as an attorney. For decades, I have handled scores of police brutality and misconduct cases — on both sides — that, often, no one else would take and some of which led to major reform;
- And as an ordinary citizen, husband and father who wants to effect change.

I have things to say. I have solutions. I have a better way for police officers to think about who they are and what they do. Too often, that blue code of silence, or seeing police work and misconduct through "blue spectacles," obscures good judgment and — so crucial to this discussion — what should be the first goal of every police-citizen encounter: that both officer and citizen live to see another day.

Instead, certain steps that can be taken by cops are not; certain attitudes that should be present are absent; certain protocols and training have not been learned or are not put into practice; and the conscious choice to do the smart thing rather than the dumb thing when face to face with tense situations vanishes in the heat of the moment. And it costs lives.

More often, the lives lost in these public, tragic encounters are not those of cops, but of those they confront. And too often the conclusion rendered in the public square is that the officer had no choice but to do what he did. He is, after all, a police officer — a "hero" who puts his life on the line every day.

To label a person a hero simply because he wears a police uniform is part of the problem. The fact is, things just aren't that simple.

Not all police are angels. Not all citizens they face on the street are villains. The police officer is just as human, and just as flawed, as the person he looks to apprehend. When it comes to human beings in volatile situations, it's always complicated. There is more than one outcome that can occur in these situations.

Obtaining the best possible outcomes begins with reexamining police culture and shifting that paradigm to a new way of looking at what can go right, rather than go wrong, if police officers approach these moments differently. Holding them up as heroes no matter what doesn't solve the problem.

As I so often say: You see a hero, I see a human being. I've begun to describe both, but there is a lot, lot more to these definitions. You'll see what I mean.

CHAPTER ONE

Police Behavior Matters

I t's all right there on the video.

Three young black men were at MotorCity Casino in Detroit and were asked by Detroit Police Department officers, whose assignment was to patrol the casino, to leave. Exactly why is unclear, but the young men later said they had not been doing anything wrong. Their accusers said they were video recording someone inside the casino, probably goofing around like just about everyone with a cell phone does these days. But apparently, this is not allowed, so the men were told to leave. Fair enough.

As the casino security camera video clearly shows, the men begin leaving the casino as ordered. The first man, Corey Proctor, heads toward the door. The second, Jeremy Smith, is not far behind. The third, Tramell Proctor, is a bit farther back because he has just cashed in his chips.

So, to repeat, the guys are doing what they were told to do. But somehow, for some officers, it isn't enough. It also bears in mind that a couple of these cops have histories of being very aggressive with people.

So they follow Corey Proctor as he heads toward the door. Then, plain as can be, one cop starts beating Corey, and another officer wallops Smith. Because Tramell Proctor is lagging, he escapes the attack. But he pulls out his cell phone and starts recording it. One of the cops sees him, dashes over to him, yanks the phone out of his hand, deletes the video and then proceeds to arrest him.

Compared to his buddies, Tramell got off easy. Smith and Corey Proctor ended up at the hospital. Proctor required surgery. Yet he and Smith were both arrested for assaulting a police officer. *What?* Those charges were dropped once authorities viewed the video — which in no way diminishes the absurdity of their arrest.

So, the question someone needs to ask — the question no one ever does ask in these situations that we hear about over and over in the news — is what did these kids do to deserve this attack? The cops later said Corey Proctor had turned around as he was approaching the exit, thus immediately becoming a threat.

Yeah, right.

For once, let's look at what the *cops* did, or failed to do.

First, they followed the young men toward the exit. Okay, they wanted assurance the young men would leave. I don't object to that, even though the fellas were doing as they were ordered. But the subsequent actions of the officers suggested their true motive — that is, to screw with them. Using the excuse that Corey turned around, thereby creating a threat, was to resort to one of the many excuses cops use to employ unwarranted force. Destroying the evidence of their conduct by deleting what Tramell recorded is further evidence of their true motives in following them out. The point is, did the cops create the threat and then use the threat they created to justify the use of force? The young men made a complaint to the department that they were victims of misconduct. But the problem is, the focus was only on *their* conduct, not on what the cops may have done to precipitate the situation. The department found no misconduct by the officers.

But it happened because the cops *chose to act* as they did. They did that because all too often, what occurs after such scenarios is exactly what unfolded here: The "investigations" afterward always focus on what the citizen allegedly did or did not do. The focus never starts with what the cops did or did not do.

That is obvious in the infamous Eric Garner case. In July 2014, Garner, who was black, died on Staten Island, New York City, after NYPD Officer

Dan Pantaleo, who is white, applied a chokehold for about 15 seconds — despite the fact that chokeholds were not permitted by the police department.

Garner was trying to sell unlicensed cigarettes on the sidewalk. The cop reached for his arm, Garner pulled away, and that's all it took for the cop, assisted by other officers, to pull him down and apply the chokehold. Garner kept saying, "I can't breathe," but it didn't matter, apparently.

His death was ruled a homicide and attracted a lot of scrutiny, sparking public demonstrations and an independent U.S. Department of Justice investigation. Milwaukee County Sheriff David Clarke Jr. testified before Congress during this investigation. His rhetoric about the Garner case tells it all. He only talked about how Garner "resisted arrest" — that Garner died of a "heart attack" and that "he wasn't choked to death." Testimonies from other sources, in my opinion, highlighted the "blue line of silence" and the reluctance or refusal by other agencies to second-guess police testimony.

Garner, 43, was a big guy. He was no saint. But on this occasion, there was no justification for what happened. The officer later was put on desk duty, but that doesn't make up for the unprovoked loss of a human life. It doesn't make up for the fact that this could have been avoided had Pantaleo, not Garner, acted differently.

How? Simple: Wait Garner out. Time was not of the essence. The mere presence of police would have shut Garner's illegal enterprise down. Garner would have no choice but to leave. Problem solved. Everybody goes home alive. Was this a "have to arrest" situation? Or was Pantaleo unwilling to exercise discretion, which escalated to a deadly force situation? That's how it looks.

The officers should have kept their distance, given Garner's size and criminal record, told him to leave and simply stayed there until he did.

This upside-down framework, this poor police behavior and the age-old police psychology that enables it, has been rolling over and over in my brain for decades now. I keep hearing all the old refrains, that the victim did this or that. Even in the rare cases when the cop's behavior comes up, it's always accompanied by the mantras, "he was only doing his duty," or "he was in fear of his life." That he was in fear because of his own inappropriate, unwarranted or just plain stupid actions never seems to come up.

This is the way things always have been. This has been the police mentality since forever.

Well, forever has to end.

It is time to shift that paradigm, so that analysis in a given situation starts with the police officer as opposed to the citizen. It is time to challenge the status quo in this nation's police department culture and mindset. No one does this. But I have decided that I must.

I have arrived at this decision after a long life of police work-related experiences — and earlier life experiences that helped shaped my attitude and sense of mission. These all began in the Motor City a long time ago.

CHAPTER TWO

What Would Perry Mason Do?

I was born in a segregated Detroit on Nov. 5, 1954. My parents were born in the South — my mother, Estella, in Kentucky, and my father, Frederick, in Tennessee. Both families later moved to Illinois, where they met; they married in 1947 after they had moved to Detroit. My father had followed my uncles, who had moved there for work. My father was a laborer, but early on in Detroit got a job as a security officer at the Civic Center, where he stayed until he retired.

I was the youngest of four Robinson children, two girls and two boys. We lived on Webb Street, a few miles north of downtown. My parents were able to purchase it — the first home they were able to buy. Back then, there were still a few white people in the neighborhood, mostly old widows. I earned money by cutting their grass, shoveling their snow and taking out their garbage.

Despite the fact that Detroit was segregated, I did not witness any ugliness regarding that scene as a youth. That probably was mainly because we didn't venture much beyond our neighborhood into the edges of the city or into the suburbs, which by definition at that time meant "no Negroes."

My environment was entirely among black citizens, other than the white teachers we had at school. But I don't recall any overt negative racial experiences in school. All of this allowed for a relatively stress-free existence — such are the fruits, for lack of a better description, of airtight segregation. The other exception was the white cops who rode in the "Big Four," elite four-man units that roamed the streets of Detroit.

My father encountered some racism connected to his job. He talked about "whitey" and how white kids would throw rocks at him when he was a kid growing up. I recall him and his brother, my Uncle Andrew, portraying the general paranoia blacks often felt when venturing beyond those airtight segregated areas. Take the time the two of them had to go to Coldwater, located in south-central Michigan. It was typical of most smaller Michigan towns: all white — and more provincial than urban Detroit to boot.

Nothing happened on this trip, but looking back, I take note of the fact that Uncle Andrew made sure to bring a gun for protection. My father also specifically mentioned being worried about being pulled over and getting killed by a white police officer. That's the way it was, and I would argue that it still is. Many black people do not feel safe in certain places, or around the people who are supposed to protect them. They never quite know what to expect.

My mother had the largest influence on me as I was growing up. She had wanted to be a lawyer, actually, a pretty amazing goal for a black woman of her generation. She did not reach this goal, but she used to watch *Perry Mason* (for younger folks, this was television's first courtroom drama) with tremendous enthusiasm. She would stand up and shout at the TV during episodes, urging Perry to defend the helpless or the victims of foul play, inequity, you name it. I was struck by this. Mom reinforced the lessons these episodes offered by encouraging hour-long family debates and discussions on religion, politics and current events. This was serious stuff to me, and I participated quite dutifully. Part of the reason I took all of these things so seriously is because I was a serious kid. I was a nerd. I liked to learn. I especially liked to learn words — big words, weird words. Language entranced me. The sound of people — yes, Perry Mason among them — waxing poetic to a selected audience resonated with me.

This may be why I was chosen at our church to recite poems, which I did with relish. Our black, conservative, nondenominational church,

Israel of God's Church, the White Horse Army, was one of the pillars of my childhood and neighborhood. I look back and realize that despite the racism of the times, I was blessed to have an intact family and good, dutiful, hard-working parents. True, we were as poor as church mice. We were typical of our community. As it relates to my later work, I can say that the two most memorable events during my young years came when Martin Luther King delivered his "I Have a Dream" speech in Detroit in 1963 in what was basically a rehearsal for his now-legendary delivery of that speech in Washington, D.C.

When word got out he was speaking downtown, it wasn't even a question for blacks in Detroit: You were going, no matter what it took. We lived some eight miles from downtown Detroit where King was to give the speech. We walked that eight miles. I'll never forget this experience and the spirit in my 8-year-old heart as we walked to hear this young, energetic, inspirational man who was approaching the height of his career. I regret I was too young to remember the speech itself.

Unfortunately, I was plenty old enough to remember a few years later, in 1968, when King was assassinated. The reaction of my all-black classmates at Hutchins Junior High School in Detroit was something I recall vividly. We all stood up, opened the windows in our classroom and proceeded to throw the chairs and desks out through them. We did it in total silence. No one said a word. It was an awesome political act, and statement, by a bunch of 13- and 14-year-olds.

The '60s were a kind of crucible for me and most others, I would say, who grew up in these times. A year before King was assassinated (which was the year Robert Kennedy was killed, and just four years after President John F. Kennedy was assassinated) brought the infamous Detroit riots of 1967.

Right after they began, I remember walking home from school and hearing the sirens, seeing the smoke and people jumping in and out of stores looting. My street was a main thoroughfare that led to the expressway. So that day, there were a lot of police cars, tons of traffic — and tanks. My parents specifically took the time to drive us around to see the areas affected by the riot, where I saw more looters. They seemed to be everywhere.

I remember cops driving around in big, black Imperials. There were usually four big white cops in those cars, with tommy guns in the back. They were "patrolling" the neighborhood. Yeah, right. We threw pears at those big cars. I'm not sure what we thought we were doing, but it reflects some early animosity and recognition of this police overreach, for sure. Life went on.

Always a good student, I entered Chadsey High School — which was half black and half white, the whites being mainly Eastern Europeans. There were never any racial problems that I recall. I did well in high school. I had one overwhelming ambition that eclipsed everything else: I wanted to be an attorney. It wasn't just *Perry Mason* and my mother's passion that directed this. It was the desire to *effect change*. Racial and other inequities were clear to me by then, and I wanted to do something about them. (Worth noting: When I was about to graduate from high school, I went to my high school counselor to discuss my future plans to become a lawyer. He promptly told me that I was setting my sights too high.)

So I didn't even wait after graduating in 1972 for the fall term to enter college, jumping right into the summer semester at Wayne State University in Detroit. I worked at a religious book store to make money; I also used to go downtown to the courts and watch lawyers doing their jobs. I talked to these guys, asked them questions. They were amazingly kind and patient with me.

In the meantime, my brother became a police officer for the Detroit Police Department. I learned through him that DPD had a cadet program for young people, and that the program paid for college. Well, that motivated me, so I applied and was accepted in 1973. This was more of a clerical kind of job — nothing like working the streets or learning police work. But you wore the uniform, learned the proper behavior and I was happy about the fact that I could get college paid for.

But the program didn't last long, unfortunately. Detroit elected its first black mayor, Coleman Young, the following year. This happened to be the first election I was eligible to vote in, and I cast my vote for this historic candidate. It was exciting, for sure, and we all supported him.

But due to budget woes, he had to cut the cadet program. Luckily, by that time, I had completed three years of college — but I had one year to finish. How to pay for it? The only option to me was to become an actual police officer, which I did in 1975. I figured I would just do the job, finish up that last college year and then go to law school. Well, life doesn't always follow our blueprints, as most of us know. My personal life was advancing, for one thing. I married Leerae, who had been my high school sweetheart, in 1976. I had to keep making a living. All told, it took me four years to finish that last year of college, but I did it. I received my bachelor's degree from Wayne State University in 1979. (Our two children, my son David Jr. and daughter Divinia, would be added to our family in 1981 and 1983.) I am proud to say all of my siblings also earned college degrees.

My experiences within the police department and in the community in the ensuing years helped shape the ideas I share in this book. For example, while attending the Detroit Police Academy, there was a white cadet who cheated, copying my work. I also helped him with other school assignments. At the time, it was just, "We're all one color: khaki." We were trying to become police officers and it was rigorous, and we counted on each other in lots of ways. So this other cadet and I sort of bonded through these experiences — or so I thought. Some years later, when we ran into each other at a baseball game, I expected a warm welcome. He completely ignored me.

Another white cop who taught at the Academy had a chip on his shoulder toward black cadets. When I finally graduated from the Academy in 1975, we were all at the graduation party. We both had the badge, right? So I said to him, in a friendly, celebrating way, "Hey, we're finally equal," and he responded coldly, "We will never be equal."

Also, after graduating from the Academy, the whole "we're all khaki" united thing disintegrated. The white cops went to one corner, the black cops to another, and that was that. It mirrored also where we all lived

— the black cops more in the city, the white ones toward the city limits, as close to those all-white suburbs as they could get. (At the time, city employees had to live in Detroit.) Certainly, there were always lots of good folks, regardless of color. There were plenty of white officers who befriended black officers and would, out of their own sense of decency, tell me what the racist white officers were doing or saying. For instance, some of those racist cops would have contests that whoever arrested the least number of blacks during a shift had to buy the beer.

All of this winds back to my purpose in examining police work, culture and even its original ideals. So it's important for the record here to share the official "Law Enforcement Code of Ethics," which all cops are supposed to a) know, and b) honor when they are doing their jobs. I was chosen to recite this code at my Police Academy graduation.

According to these ethics, I and my fellow officers swore that:

"As a law enforcement officer, my fundamental duty is to serve mankind; to safeguard lives and property; to protect the innocent against deception, the weak against oppression or intimidation and the peaceful against violence or disorder; and to respect the constitutional rights of all to liberty, equality and justice.

"I will keep my private life unsullied as an example to all and will behave in a manner that does not bring discredit to me or my agency. I will maintain courageous calm in the face of danger, scorn or ridicule; develop self-restraint; and be constantly mindful of the welfare of others. Honest in thought and deed both in my personal and official life, I will be exemplary in obeying the law and the regulations of my department. Whatever I see or hear of a confidential nature or that is confided in me in my official capacity will be kept ever secret unless revelation is necessary in the performance of my duty.

"I will never act officiously or permit personal feelings, prejudices, political beliefs, aspirations, animosities or friendships to influence my decisions. With no compromise for crime and with relentless prosecution of criminals, I will enforce the law courteously and appropriately without fear or favor, malice or ill will, never employing unnecessary force or

violence and never accepting gratuities.

"I recognize the badge of my office as a symbol of public faith, and I accept it as a public trust to be held so long as I am true to the ethics of police service. I will never engage in acts of corruption or bribery, nor will I condone such acts by other police officers. I will cooperate with all legally authorized agencies and their representatives in the pursuit of justice.

"I know that I am responsible for my own standard of professional performance and will take every reasonable opportunity to enhance and improve my level of knowledge and competence.

"I will constantly strive to achieve these objectives and ideals, dedicating myself (before God) to my chosen profession — law enforcement."

Such was our commission as police officers. Sure, it's a tall order, as is any such code. But it doesn't look unachievable to anyone who just wants to do right and try hard to treat all human beings as, yeah, *human beings*. How well we conducted ourselves according to these ethics? Well, that's another story, as I soon would discover.

CHAPTER THREE

Seeing Citizens as People First

Code of ethics notwithstanding, once out on the job, I saw my share of police misconduct — most notably, citizens getting beaten up when there was no call for it. I did not report it at the time because no one was hurt badly enough to be sent to the hospital. (I'll be addressing people not getting to the hospital later.)

And I was part of the police culture. You did not rat out your fellow cops. In retrospect, I regret this. But I was young, dutiful and, I guess you could say, brainwashed. As for my own conduct, especially in the light of many officers' tendency to be too aggressive too soon, I had a different impulse. On my first call, I was dispatched to a couple's house for a domestic dispute. This couple was in their 60s, and they were getting physical with one another. I was all of 21 years old, thinking, "What's my response here?" The instinct would be to dictate, perhaps even with some physicality: "Get your ass over here, sit down, and you here, you do the same!" That could have worked, to a point. But would it have resolved the issue? Probably not. Might it agitate things? Likely, yes. So I thought, I'll embarrass these people, make them rethink their ways.

"How old are you now? How long have you been married?" I asked. "I know you love each other. You're fussing and fighting and calling me to referee. I'm 21 years old! You've been married longer than I've been alive. I'm about to get married. I should be looking to *you* for advice."

I went on like this and before long, they were kissing and hugging. I did my job. I upheld the law as I had sworn to do. But instead of making a situation worse, I tried to defuse it. They didn't teach this in the Academy. I guess it was just an instinct, and a level of compassion. The fact that I had had a good upbringing helped, and maybe my temperament did, too. What also certainly made a difference was that I'd had three years of college by then. I saw citizens, even those I arrested or addressed in tense situations, as people first. They were just like me: vulnerable.

Education had provided maturity, the ability to take that first step: Stop and think, and *then* act. I will have much to say about this going forward. But all too often, police recruits only had high school diplomas or a G.E.D. Police departments had no choice but to accept such recruits because that was who applied. Police work was seen as a blue-collar profession — one that not many would pursue in any case. Departments had to work with what they had.

This is one area that should be changed. You can't expect uneducated youngsters to have wisdom, especially in volatile or complicated situations that require quick decisions. More education, some college, would help. Certainly, the best advice I ever got as I went on with my police work came from another black officer. He told me, "Treat people in the street with respect, because you never know when you might need them." I learned again and again that those were truly words to live by. Even a bad person can save your life. I also had another official document, along with the aforementioned Code of Ethics, to guide me. It is a U.S. Department of Justice document called "The Use-of-Force Continuum." The definition of "use of force" is "the levels, or continuum, of force police use includ(ing) basic verbal and physical restraint, less-than-lethal force and lethal force."

The first of several steps on this continuum is *"Officer Presence — no force is used. Considered the best way to resolve a situation."* Just the presence of an officer often deters or defuses a crime; officers are supposed to be professional and non-threatening.

This step opens up an entire psychological conversation, one that it would behoove those in police work to think long and hard about. It centers on a fundamental irony about human behavior: What distinguishes the citizen from the cop is what they actually share in common. Both are human beings. But in confrontational situations, both are unwilling to recognize the other's humanity.

What must happen — with the assistance, I hope, of the suggestions and observations in this book — is that the cop and the citizen recognize their own abilities and inabilities, and that both are likely frightened to at least some degree. It's like, "I'm scared and you're scared, too." But instead, the cop often doesn't realize how much he is scaring the citizen, and vice versa. Citizens often fail to recognize that cops can be scared, too. To expand on this dynamic: Human interaction occurs in all relationships, of course, not just those in police-citizen encounters.

Certain people occupy certain positions of power; police officers are chief among them. And as a cop, you need to understand how to use this assumed power, to use it in an effective — not lethal — manner. You remember that the citizen in front of you is human and scared, just like you. As an officer, I knew I had this advantage over people and recognized how it operated. I remembered how I felt years before when I was stopped by cops: The heart starts beating furiously, as in a fight-or-flight mode. So if I remember this, then I'm in the driver's seat, as long as I don't abuse my position of power. If a person is feeling fearful, and I know that, then I don't have to do more than walk up slowly to them most of the time. I can use my benevolent psychological advantage in my interactions with citizens. Instead of acting forcefully, I exhibit courtesy and respect — something that the citizen doesn't expect — and that immediately disarms his mentality.

Officers are the ones who set the stage of any encounter. Recognizing that the citizen, regardless of their outer behavior, is afraid, I don't want to do anything that will increase that fear. So I use that fear, essentially, to keep my own actions in check, resolve the situation and allow both of us to go home that day.

Officers need to approach citizens with respect and courtesy, always. This relates to the second step on the Use-of-Force Continuum:

"Verbalization — force is not-physical." Ideally, the officer asks very calmly and politely for information or, say, someone's license. They can increase volume if needed.

Now, let's stop here for a moment and consider the case of Willie Hamilton of Detroit, a man I represented as an attorney. The scene, once again, is at a casino, and is similar to the previous case I described. It was also on video. Hamilton has been asked to leave. He does so, but he is doing it on his terms. That's largely because, one, he's handicapped and cannot walk normally, and two, Willie Hamilton was by God's making a very frustrating, annoying individual. He had attitude to go along with his walk. This reinforces a basic reality for cops: You can't pick and choose the people you come into contact with. Throw in other variables such as volatile or uncontrollable conditions and a cop's own deficiencies — quick temper, bias, racism or just stupidity — and bad or crazy things can happen.

The fact that Hamilton is annoying is irrelevant, or should be. In any case, casino security only can escort someone so far from the casino itself; after that, police take over. So as Hamilton is leaving, a big white cop comes up and tells him, gruffly, to do what he's already doing — albeit in his own shuffling, with-attitude way.

The cop technically has the authority to issue this command — though that he does so even as Hamilton is already doing it, and in an unfriendly tone, tells me the cop is already out of line. So it's no surprise that the cop starts pushing Hamilton, then begins to beat him. It's all on camera — again. (What part of "there are cameras *everywhere* these days" don't these cops understand?) The cop essentially became angry because Hamilton was, well, Hamilton — annoying. But he was also *human*, that psychological factor the cop failed to take into consideration. This reinforces the basic goal that a police officer has to have a natural talent of discernment in order to effectively and lawfully carry out his authority. Why did this cop get so mad? There's no rational justification. He's an angry cop. So Hamilton gets beat up.

Along with the cop's failure to employ psychology in this situation, the moral to this story is that the beginning of this interaction should have occurred long before the cop pushed Hamilton. He should have looked at Hamilton in the distance, and assessed how to help Hamilton leave, if that was even necessary, and to keep in mind his restrictions. In other words, he can follow Willie Hamilton as far as he wants to as long as he's satisfied Hamilton is leaving. This is Step One on the Use-of-Force Continuum: Officer Presence. Make sure the guy leaves. Do your job, which is to enforce the law. That's the goal, it's always the goal, but don't let unguided thinking mess everything up, i.e., an angry, unprovoked cop beats the crap out of a handicapped man who has done nothing wrong. This case received considerable press coverage.

Here's another, more severe example that occurred in November 2014. This presses home further what can happen when cops fail to remember basic psychology — when they don't wait and think before acting.

Tamir Rice, a 12-year-old black youth in Cleveland, Ohio, was sitting on a swing in a city park and pointing what looked like a gun at people, as the dispatch call to police characterized it. The caller twice said the gun was probably "a fake" and that the "shooter" was "probably a juvenile." This information apparently was not relayed adequately to the two officers who responded to the call; we may never know for sure whether it was or was not. The officers make their way to the park. In seconds, they spot the subject and see him appear to grab at his waistband for a gun. The cops fire two shots, and presto, the kid takes a bullet. He dies the next day.

What is immediately obvious after the shooting is that this is a kid. And guess what else? *The gun was a replica. It was a fake — a toy, essentially.*

What makes this all the more troubling is that one of the cops — the one who fired the shots — had been deemed *as a recruit* to be unstable and unfit for duty, according to reports after the shooting.

You're asking, unstable or not, how were the cops supposed to know the gun was a toy? Good question. They weren't, in those two seconds that passed before they fired. But had they reacted differently before even reaching the scene, Tamir Rice would not have died. (Subsequent "investigations" by authorities did not recommend indictment; the Rice family sued and won $6 million.) Let's recast this scene, employing a better decision-making process.

So, I am with my partner in the patrol car. We get the dispatch call on the police radio — the kind of call that instantly causes concern: "Male with a gun in a park." The first instinct is to let all the bad police stuff kick in. Resist the instinct. *Think.*

We're, say, at least a few miles away. We have a great asset with us right now, before we even get to the scene: *THE RADIO*. This is my lifeline, and if I need help, I can get it, so I need to keep an open line of communication at all times. So there's a man with a gun. What goes on in my mind? Number One, I'm a police officer. Number Two, I've got a job to do. But my mind shouldn't stop there. I should ask: What are my limitations? I'm not all-powerful. If I think I am, I put the subject's life, and mine, in danger.

Once again, we're both scared. I don't want to be one of those officers who has to (or claim they had to) make a "split-second decision" if I can avoid it. And in fact, I can avoid it. First, if I keep talking to the dispatcher, I likely learn that the caller said the gun is probably a fake and that the subject probably is a juvenile. How can the caller discern that? *Because this is happening in the middle of the afternoon; it is broad daylight.*

Next, to avoid that split-second pressure, to give myself more time, do I turn on the blue lights and siren, get to the scene and rush over to the "man" with the "gun"? Well, no, because that's not smart, and because I may know by now it's probably a kid and possibly a replica, not a real gun. Flashing bright lights, sirens and charging after someone only inflames a situation by increasing the fear factor all the more and inciting a hasty response by me, the kid or both of us. But these cops followed a different path. And we know the result. The police dash cam clearly shows it.

In Freudian psychology, the common phrase "Freudian slip" refers to an inadvertent mistake in speech or writing that is thought to reveal a person's unconscious motives, wishes or attitudes. One interesting, possible insight into the cops' behavior is a kind of Freudian slip/moment: The cops rushed up to Rice because they could, in fact, see — or knew ahead of time — that he was just a kid. They approached closely because it was a non-threatening situation, not the opposite. What if they had followed those first two steps? Police presence — at a safe distance and, so key, *inside the scout car*, where the officer is safer and can, also key, use the vehicle's public address unit to employ the "Verbalization" step: "Son, you need to put that gun down."

It's so important to remember that the scout car is part of the police presence. So there is no initial need to jump out, rush up to or toward a person who you should remember is already scared and presumed to be armed. Again, in the police investigation of this tragedy, no indictment was called for. Admittedly, these are not easy circumstances. No one argues that.

What I'm emphasizing is that case by tragic case, we can learn more from what wasn't done than what was done by the officers. Prevailing age-old psychology in police officers and in departments helps ensure the wrong path, the stupid path, the split-second, don't-think path. A lot of this goes back to the hero/human being dichotomy: I need to act human to be perceived by citizens as one. Playing the "hero" role is not the answer. In fact, the whole "hero" thing needs to be reframed entirely. Believe it or not, it doesn't help cops when most people assume they're heroes; it hinders them.

CHAPTER FOUR

Authority Versus Power

I call the tendency for people to assume cops are heroes the "Police Mystic."

This mystic relates to the conviction that being a police officer is fraught with danger, excitement, allure, intrigue, grittiness, gore, reality, sensuality, threat and everything else Hollywood puts on the screen. In reality, cops have a job that borders on being boring. But many cops find themselves needing to live up to the hype. In fairness, the public's perception of police puts a burden on them, which sets them apart from other public servants. Judges, juries, citizens, lawyers and other common folks give cops a certain latitude in their behavior that a city bus driver, for example, would never enjoy.

We see it in opinions of most judges in their rulings on issues of immunity. (I will get to that dynamic later.) We see it in jury verdicts of "no cause" when the police officer convinces the jury he only had that split second to make a life-or-death decision. We see it in average citizens when they consider, but hesitate, to make a formal complaint after an officer rudely confronts them, detains them, never apologizes and then sends them on their way. So as society routinely hails police officers as heroes, police officers follow suit, and are understandably prone to viewing themselves as heroes. This puts a lot of pressure on a cop, who now has to act like a hero. That's a highly combustible dictate, since any two people can disagree on what constitutes a "hero" and what conditions warrant "heroic" behavior. This can lead cops, acting on their interpretation of "hero," to abuse their power. The crucial aspect to this dichotomy of hero versus human being brings up the integral dynamic of power versus authority.

Lawfully, police officers are given the authority, *not the power*, to act. Police — along with the public, juries, judges — too often confuse power for authority, which too often leads to unsatisfactory to tragic outcomes.

Let me give you an example of an actual case where a judge used the words "authority" and "power" interchangeably — and thus, incorrectly. He ruled that "police officers occupy a unique position of trust in our society. They are responsible for enforcing the law and protecting society from criminal acts. They are given the authority to detain, to arrest and, when necessary, to use deadly force. As visible symbols of that formidable power, an officer is furnished a distinctively marked car, a uniform, a badge and a gun. Those who challenge an officer's action do so at their peril; anyone who resists an officer's proper exercise of authority or who obstructs the performance of an officer's duty is subject to criminal prosecution."

The reality is: Police officers are charged to act only with the authority granted them by the state or authorizing entity. For example, the official Use-of-Force guidelines for members of the Detroit Police Department state:

"Police officers are armed with the legal authority to use proper force necessary to lawfully arrest citizens. However, this authority is one that is strictly limited by the laws of the state and the rules and policies of the department."

It's important to note that nowhere in the DPD Use-of-Force policy is the word "power." Most police department policies are careful not to use the terms interchangeably. The department policy describes the officer's authority as "strictly limited."

Nevertheless, the abuse of power, rather than judicious use of authority, continues. And there are certain groups of people who tend to be victims of the abuse of authority. They aren't just African Americans, but others who are rendered powerless by society in one way or another: the poor, the culturally isolated, the mentally ill and mentally disabled, the very young, the uneducated, females. Therefore, the abusive police officer has an array of potential victims.

Consider a recent case in Los Angeles County. A heavyset woman with a history of mental illness and aggression toward people boards a bus. Two cops immediately try to get her off. There is good reason based on her past behavior on buses that prompts this action. One witness even reported she became physical with the cops. But that doesn't justify what the cops do.

They immediately start cursing at her. She cusses back. Citizens cussing at cops is hardly unusual. The cops, however, don't decide just to ignore this behavior, which would have been the smartest and easiest response. Nor do they try to defuse the situation by talking to her, or just waiting to let her calm down. No, instead, one of the cops just ups and coldcocks her — right there. And right where a passenger captured it all on video using his cell phone.

This lady didn't do anything wrong. True, like Willie Hamilton, she was rough and unlikeable, to say the least. She was also homeless and had a long history of mental illness, including aggressive behavior. These people don't vie for Ms. or Mr. Congeniality, right? But the cop was unnecessarily combative with her. To explain: Every city has a "disorderly" statute that gives cops the right to ask someone who is being disorderly to leave the premises — in this case, the bus. The woman was having none of it, essentially claiming, "I don't have to leave. I paid my fare, I can do what I want." The cop has the *authority* to say, "No, ma'am, you don't." He has the authority to remove her, yes. But it's when and how that matter.

He crosses the line big time when he punches her. It's his job, his challenge, to operate within the confines of *authority*, not power. He has to find a way. That's the constraint cops face, and they blow it all the time. I referred earlier to the first two steps of The Use-of-Force Continuum: Officer Presence and Verbalization, when officers can, if polite tones don't work, increase their volume or shorten commands to help gain compliance from a subject.

This should have been enough for the cops on the bus, especially given this was a woman with special needs. But they at least could have resorted to the first part of the third Use-of-Force step, "Empty-Hand Control," which is the "soft technique." This is when officers use "grabs, holds and joint locks to restrain an individual." I argue that even this was entirely unnecessary. But the cops jumped right to the second part of step three: "Hard technique. Officers use punches and kicks to restrain an individual."

It was all on video, which should have been damning enough. But videos seldom are. Every time there's a video on the TV news showing police officers doing something bad, the response is, "Not all cops are bad." True. And even this cop on the bus is a good cop, too, because on the next run, he may very well save someone from a burning car.

There were no legal consequences in this case. The woman was put on mental health observation for a time and was released. No action was taken against the officers. So it all goes nowhere. The entire line of reasoning is irrelevant. Forget this good cop/bad cop back-and-forth. These labels don't serve a purpose. It always goes back to the human being — me, you and everyone. But first, and foremost, *me*.

One experience I had drives this home. My partner and I were responding to a call from an elderly woman whose adult schizophrenic 20-something son had gone off his medications. He was bonkers. While he wasn't violent or a threat, he was acting crazy and she needed us to get him to the hospital psychiatric ward. This is not an uncommon occurrence. We call this a "transport" call.

My partner happened to be a very skinny guy (we were both also in our 20s). I was 5-foot-9 and about 175 pounds at that point. The schizophrenic young man was 6-foot-3, about 240 pounds, muscle-bound, and as we later learned, had wrists that were too big for our handcuffs.

So, my skinny-as-a-rail partner and I go into the house. The young man is sitting just inches from his TV screen, holding a blaring radio up to his ear. The volume on both radio and TV is turned all the way up. He's tapping his foot like crazy. But that's all. My partner approaches him first, quickly, and says bluntly, roughly, "Get up. You're going to jail." Well, the young man ignores him. He just keeps doing what he's doing, totally in his own world.

My partner gets more aggressive and makes a move toward the guy, who suddenly stands up and lunges his entire body toward my partner. My partner freaks and retreats out to the porch. (I totally don't blame him.) While I give him credit at least for not doing something like pulling his gun, I'm thinking, "But how in the hell can I help this little old lady who has called 911 for help? How can I do this without making things worse? How am I going to get this guy out of the house and not risk my safety or his, though given the size imbalance, I was the likely victim of any skirmish. After all, this young man isn't a criminal, *he's mentally ill*. The poor youth is crazy, and his poor mother lives with him, cares for him."

So, my partner has fled; the young man returns to what he was doing — the TV, radio, tapping his foot again, the volume way up. And I just start doing the same thing: I sit down next to him, start tapping my foot — just as frantically as he is; I'm matching what he is doing. I literally put my hand up, as if I had a radio, playing like I'm enjoying whatever it is that he's enjoying. And eventually, after a couple of long minutes, the guy reaches over, turns the TV and radio down. And we start talking. Then he stands up, I stand up, and say softly, with the compassion I felt for him, "You gotta come with us." He nods, and calmly walks out to the police car.

See what I'm saying? It was the human I saw, and it was a human I had to be. My reaction was tempered with compassion. They don't teach you this in the Academy, but perhaps this example will help. And the mentally ill citizen is complicated. They aren't "stupid." They can be plenty smart. But so often, they begin with one train of thought, then wind into another, and are unable to return to a typical thinking pattern. In the fable, Hansel and Gretel leave a trail of breadcrumbs behind them as they journey through the woods, in order to find the way back. But the breadcrumbs are eaten. Likewise, for many mentally ill people, the breadcrumbs behind them — their thinking patterns — vanish, and they can't find their way back. You have to reach your hand out and show them the way.

It bears noting that in the cases I bring up, tragedy has resulted after cops fail to analyze situations consistent with what they are required, and allowed, to do by virtue of their given authority. They end up increasing the danger to themselves, which forces them to protect themselves, which leads to bad actions, which they then have to justify. And in these cases, that's what the cops do — justifying their actions by citing the danger they faced.

They don't say they created the danger to begin with. And I allege that in my experience, cops and police departments know about this creation of danger chain reaction. They know but don't care. They consistently advance through the Use-of-Force Continuum, not step by step. Of course, the rules allow cops to skip steps if circumstances warrant. But often, a cop does that anyway, partially motivated by the knee-jerk mental belief that by the time he calculates which step he should employ, he'll be dead.

When it comes time to examine this behavior, the public is just as reluctant to second-guess cops as the cops themselves are. It's the whole "I'm risking my life to save yours, so I don't need you to second-guess me" thing. So, people don't, and thus the normal feedback that would check many of these overreaches doesn't occur. It is blocked by fear and guilt of not backing cops 100 percent.

For the record, the rest of the Use-of-Force Continuum steps, after the "Officer Presence" and Verbalization," both of which do not call for use of force, are:

- *Empty-Hand Control — Officers use bodily force to gain control of a situation.* This is the use of grabs, holds and joint locks or, if needed, punches and kicks to restrain individuals;
- *Less-Lethal Methods — Officers use less-lethal technologies to gain control of a situation.* This includes blunt impact via use of a baton or projectile; chemical sprays or projectiles; or the use of "high-voltage,

low-amperage jolt of electricity at a distance"; and

- *Lethal Force — officers use lethal weapons to gain control of a situation. Should only be used if a suspect poses a serious threat to the officer or another individual.* In other words, this is the use of firearms.

  Notice the steps don't include "coldcock when necessary."

I was a police officer for 13 years, until 1988. Despite the less-than-positive aspects, I wouldn't trade having done the work. It taught me a lot. And it helped me when I began to deal with police officers and administrators in court — which I began to do after getting my law degree from the Detroit College of Law in 1985. It was then that I began my first work as a lawyer, during those last three years at DPD. The learning about all-things-cop picked up speed.

CHAPTER FIVE

Crossing 'the Blue Line'

A s I was waiting for the results of my bar exam, I put in for a transfer to DPD's Legal Advisor Unit. This unit consisted of staff attorneys (or cops with law licenses) whose job it was to represent the interests of the Detroit Police Department, the Chief of Police and the City of Detroit. I knew this would give me much-needed experience. And I was attracted by the idea of the law as the sacrosanct instrument that worked for the betterment of society.

In other words, the process would be fair to all sides, come what may.

How naïve.

One of my first assignments was to be on call to answer formal questions that the Detroit City Council had for the Chief of Police. I don't remember what the area of inquiry was, but I was instructed, as I sat at my desk, to wait for direction. At some point, I would be told whether to go to City Council and, if I went, what to say and how to say it. That was my first reality check on what I had gotten myself into. It was politics.

I learned a lot more as time went on. My job was to advocate for DPD's position, no matter what it was. We very often got public records requests from lawyers under the Freedom of Information Act (FOIA). I would argue on behalf of the department; for the most part, we didn't want to give up records.

Michigan law delineates certain records that we did not have to give up. But in all cases, my job was to hand over as few records as possible to lawyers. They in turn would file lawsuits to challenge these denials. It was all part of the game, to a large extent.

But it was a rigged game, I soon observed. Judges generally sided with our refusal to release records. They did so under a cloak of secrecy, privilege, privacy, confidentiality — all code words for denying release of records we didn't want out there. So all I had to do was spew those words and the response was almost automatic. Screw the public's right to know.

Well, the public did, and does, have the right to know, which is why we have laws protecting that right. In a perfect world, it's a balancing act between that right and what is truly, and appropriately, confidential. But I saw over and over that many judges never got close to that balance in their zealous deference to the police department lawyer and the department itself.

Out in the suburbs, where you had mostly white judges, there was even greater deference to a cop's word than in the City of Detroit courtrooms.

As for my own personal career path, I defended a couple of officers on trial for police brutality, and the victims won. I realized what litigating the other side could bring: satisfaction in effecting change, my original mission, and, I will be honest, a much better income — if you knew what you were doing.

But for the time being, I was on the police team. And the mentality shared by officers and the lawyers representing them in court exposed to me how the system really was rigged to favor the police department.

There was a mentality and a way of doing things that encouraged cops to stick to the cop culture. For instance, let's say it's October 2011. Officers get involved in an arrest, and the guy who gets arrested is beaten. The cops bring him into the station and he goes before the desk supervisor, who has the responsibility of looking at every arrested person, presumably to see any evidence of injury and to make sure all is kosher. This is an attempt to benefit the guy and police officers in the process.

What really happens is that the cops go to their computers and proceed to write up their police reports. These reports use a formula we all knew well. It goes something like, "We received a radio run of a man creating a disturbance ... Upon writer's arrival, we approach John Doe ... Writer attempted to restrain John Doe, who resisted. Writer's use of force was necessary to effect arrest ..." Throw in the birth date, address and whatnot, and presto! The Police Report is completed.

Meanwhile, John Doe is standing there, all bloody. What he has said has melted away in minutes, and it certainly can't compete with The Police Report. These reports become etched in stone. A year later, when John Doe gets out of jail, he hires a lawyer. He tells the lawyer the officers beat him up. The lawyer files suit.

I get the case as the department attorney. I get the report, which was and remains immutable. This is the story, it is the record, and when I ask the cops what happened, the response is, "It's just like the report says." End of interview. Whoa.

So I have to give legs to this defense. How do I do that? The cops who whupped John Doe don't tolerate me, as their lawyer, second-guessing them. That is all part of that cop culture. It's not allowed. I can read the report and run with it. In my view by now, this renders that original report little more than street-corner justice.

But as the DPD lawyer, I have to portray the plaintiff as the bad guy. I have to find out all this stuff about this guy the cops didn't know about him, even when they arrested and beat him up. I find out and relay that, for instance, this guy was arrested five years ago for breaking and entering, he's been in trouble since day one, etc.

That's how I defend and uphold the year-old police report. Not by questioning the officers who wrote it — about why the guy had to get beat up, why there isn't much detail in the report about that. I just take it as gospel. I know that's what I am supposed to do. That's how I give legs to the lie. No one else questions the story, either.

When these cases came to court, I learned I had the advantage when defending cops. One plaintiff's lawyer put it this way: We're like Picasso. We have to paint a pretty picture. Then the cop's lawyer throws mud at it: "Did you just get convicted five years ago? Did your wife file for divorce after accusing you of abuse? Do you have two DUIs?" And so on.

More integral to this institutional inequity is the automatic deference many — but not all — judges give to police officers. Who was governor in Michigan affected the judicial temperament and exercise of legal discretion. For instance, 12 years of Gov. John Engler resulted in the alteration of the landscape of how justice was dispensed in Michigan. Judges appointed by Engler had a judicial philosophy that leaned heavily toward police officers.

They overwhelmingly give credence to anything police officers say. When I was a DPD lawyer, these kinds of judges just about fell over themselves to follow my lead, my case. Cops knew this. They knew they could get away with what they had done. They knew the judges had their back, essentially.

This symbiosis infected what was supposed to be an impartial process of justice. This was all part of the culture. This dynamic between cops and judges was especially present out in the suburbs, but there were plenty of cases in Detroit.

Luckily, there were some judges who didn't cater to this nonsense. I remember Recorder's Court Judge Henry Heading, who spoke at our police academy graduation. He told us, "You've got a tough job, and I will support you in all your endeavors. But don't come in my courtroom and lie. If you do, you will suffer my wrath. Do. Not. Lie."

A lot of city judges were progressive and less automatically deferential to cops. You never knew until you showed up in court which kind of judge you would get. But that so many were part of the cop culture was not a positive thing.

All of this rubbed me the wrong way. I also was getting restless professionally. I was ready to open my own law practice, so I established David Robinson & Associates in 1986. I was only part time at first, still handling some cases for DPD. But by 1988, I was making enough money, even part time, to finally walk away from police work entirely.

I had learned a lot, and was grateful for the opportunities I had as a DPD officer and lawyer. I also was in the position of knowing the place inside-out — how it worked, all the excuses, assumptions, rigged outcomes. I was ready to defect to the other side of the blue line.

CHAPTER SIX

'Probably Caused' Doesn't Cut It

O ne major tenet of the law as it relates to police work, especially to beatings, is a phrase we all have heard and probably think we understand: "Probable cause."

But my work indicated otherwise, and this concept was one that I especially focused on when I taught police recruits at the Detroit Police Academy. It was crucial that these future officers learn and develop a full appreciation for the role of probable cause in police work.

Few cops I ever knew got it right. I can say that in over 30 years of litigating cases, I never heard the right answer in depositions with cops when I asked them to define "probable cause." They would respond that they arrest someone because that person's actions aroused suspicion. They'd say, "You're suspicious about a person by the way they act," or some similar response.

Probable cause is far more sweeping in its protection of the American citizen. It is a fundamental right, guaranteed in the United States Constitution. The Detroit Police Manual defines it this way:

When Probable Cause is Required

All felony arrests, whether or not pursuant to an arrest warrant, must be based upon probable cause. Even when an arrest warrant has been issued, the person arrested may later claim in court that the arrest was based on insufficient probable cause. If a court determines that a probable cause was lacking, any evidence found in a search incident to that arrest will have to be suppressed … However, the officer will not be subject to civil damages for making an illegal arrest pursuant to a warrant that appeared valid on its face. Probable cause is not sufficient to make an arrest for a misdemeanor unless otherwise stipulated by statutory provisions.

Defining and Determining Probable Cause

To a large extent, probable cause is a question of common sense. Although the term lacks precise definition, it suggests either a probability, or at least a very substantial possibility, that the person to be arrested has committed a crime. In weighing the facts to determine whether probable cause exists, the officer may draw reasonable inferences that can be supported by his previous experiences as an officer; that is, the officer need not view the facts in the same manner as would a layperson not experienced in law enforcement. It must be emphasized, however, that probable cause must be based upon concrete facts. Mere suspicion, rumor or anonymous information without supported facts will not suffice to establish cause.

Think about it: Our American democratic concept of "freedom" can be yanked away at a moment's notice by young Officer John Doe wearing his badge if he decides he has "probable cause" to arrest or detain someone. If he doesn't fully understand this concept, or misconstrues it, the consequences to citizens can be devastating.

Extrapolation from a poor understanding or abuse of probable cause can eventually result in a wrongful conviction and jail, prison or, in some states, the death penalty for a completely innocent human being.

So it is absolutely essential that officers understand the responsibility they have not in *depriving* a person's freedom, but in *protecting* it by proper use of the power of "probable cause"-based arrests. In other words, it's not "probably caused," folks.

One case in which I was part of the litigation team is a good example of probable cause abuse. This involved a man named Eddie Joe Lloyd, who confessed to a murder and rape of a 14-year-old that he never committed. How in the world did that happen?

Eddie lived much of his life in a Detroit psychiatric facility. He was a nice guy, a really nice guy. True, he was psychotic, but he was a good, decent man who tried to do his best.

Back in the 1980s in Detroit, there was a rash of schoolgirl rapes and murders. It was frightening, and a lot of pressure was put on Mayor Coleman Young and the DPD to solve and ultimately stop these crimes.

So Eddie Joe Lloyd, a 50-something black man sitting in the psych ward, volunteered himself to help the police solve the crime. I am not sure why. But he wrote a letter to the DPD saying he had information that could help solve these crimes.

DPD sent a detective over to interview him. They talked to him *four different times*, each with no witness and no recording — nothing but Eddie and a police detective who was very practiced in the art of interrogation. By the end of the fourth interview, Eddie confessed to the rape and murder of one of the girls.

It was one of the greatest abuses of authority by a police detective that exists. Here we had a man who is psychotic, who lived his life in and out of psychiatric facilities. I learned in my subsequent work on this case that through the course of these unrecorded, unwitnessed interrogations, the detective fed facts that had not been released to the public to Eddie, which Eddie repeated back to him.

These statements were then "attributed" to Eddie, though there was no way prior to this he could have known these details. It didn't matter. Slam-dunk. Eddie spent the next 17-plus years in jail.

While Eddie was mentally ill, he wasn't stupid. In jail, he saw a program about the Innocence Project, which helped wrongfully convicted people. The people from this group took his case, and contacted me as a local lawyer who could assist with it. I readily agreed, serving as co-counsel.

This was in 1985-1986. At that time, DNA evidence was coming into its own as a major tool in criminal investigation. Long story short, DNA evidence proved that Eddie was innocent. His DNA had not been present at the scene of the crime.

Now, prosecutors contend that just because someone's DNA is absent from a scene doesn't prove a person wasn't there. This is true, technically. But also true is they can't prove he was there, either. And I've already described the interrogation abuse used against him.

Eddie was released, his conviction overturned in 2002. We then filed suit against the officers, DPD and City of Detroit. We won not just money, but much more importantly, we forced the implementation of a new requirement that all interrogations for serious crimes be recorded. This case received significant coverage in the media.

It was rewarding to help poor Eddie, and we were glad to have won this case and effect change. But it was not the only probable cause case I've handled, unfortunately.

On May 8, 2016, Arthur Chapman, a 26-year-old black man, was driving along I-94 in the Detroit suburb of Allen Park. His 2010 black Dodge Challenger had a white stripe across its front hood and a license plate reading "SHAKAZ." He was not driving erratically, speeding or impaired. He was just like you and me driving down the road thinking all is well, and we'll get to our destination as planned.

A good young man, Arthur earned a degree from Eastern Michigan University and had a full-time job as a supervisor at one of the casinos in Detroit, overseeing 40 employees and earning $55,000 a year.

That May 8, he was going to pick up his great uncle to take him to the airport — just an ordinary, nice man doing a favor for a family member on what should have been an ordinary day. But that day changed his life in many ways.

Out of nowhere comes a cop, Officer D. Mack of the Allen Park Police Department. Mack is white.

Mack had been sitting in his patrol car on the side of the expressway. A car zoomed past him going 91 miles per hour, swerving from one lane to another and even blowing by a few cars along the right shoulder. Clearly, this was a reckless driver. This person was driving a gray 2015 Dodge Challenger — a five-year difference in vehicle design, and a contrasting color that anyone would easily see.

The speeding vehicle clearly was not Arthur. But that didn't seem to matter to Mack.

As Arthur drove by Mack's location well after the real reckless driver had — Arthur never even saw that vehicle, they were that far apart on the highway — Mack pulled him over, siren on, lights blaring. And that's when Arthur's nightmare began.

This is what actually happened. I'll follow this with what Mack said happened, and how it helps indicate his total disregard for probable cause.

As soon as Arthur saw the police car behind him, he obeyed the law, pulling over and stopping on the right shoulder. Once again, a citizen complying dutifully.

Mack didn't seem to see it that way. He stomped toward Arthur's car and ordered him to drop his car keys out the window. Arthur did so. Mack then approached the window, his gun raised. He told Arthur to get out of the car. Arthur did so, immediately disclosing that he had a concealed weapons permit (CPL), which the law requires him to do, and that he had a gun beneath his seat.

Mack replied gruffly, ordering Arthur to unclasp his seat belt and telling him that as long as he didn't go for the gun, *he wouldn't shoot him*. Whoa. Nice. Put the kid at ease, officer.

Here this young man was complying 100 percent, and even disclosing as required that he had a gun, but Mack was already going commando.

As soon as Arthur removed his seat belt, Mack dragged him out of the car, though Arthur was already getting out on his own. Mack immediately spun Arthur around and handcuffed him so hard, Arthur's fingers and hands began to numb up.

So far, despite all this, Arthur did not resist arrest. Still, he was treated roughly for doing absolutely nothing wrong. Suffice it to say, Arthur was feeling anxious and helpless.

Mack said he was arresting Arthur for reckless driving. What? Arthur instantly told Mack, several times, that he had the wrong guy, and he should not have pulled him over; he was going 70 miles per hour, the speed limit! Mack ignored him. Arthur also repeated several times that the handcuffs were too tight. Mack ignored that, too, and hauled Arthur to the police station. He had Arthur's car towed.

Mack then sat down to write his report, making stuff up in order to create probable cause for Arthur's arrest.

He wrote that he saw the license plate of the speeding vehicle, which he said he kept in his sight until pulling it over. He said the license plate of the car going 91 miles per hour read "SHAKAZ." He also reported that Arthur admitted to being the driver of the gray, speeding Challenger.

Mack had to write these total falsehoods to establish probable cause. But, as I reported in the lawsuit we filed later, "Mack couldn't arrest Arthur merely because he had a dark-colored Dodge vehicle … It is not a crime to have a dark-colored Dodge vehicle. A reasonable inference is that after Mack lost sight of the speeding vehicle, he just continued eastbound on I-94 until he saw some vehicle that was similar to the speeder. That is not sufficient for probable cause to stop or to arrest a person." Arthur never got close to saying he was driving the speeding Challenger.

So, how to reconcile two completely different stories?

We rely, once again, ladies and gentlemen, on the "there are cameras everywhere, doofus" element.

A man named Mina Fahp happened to be on the road at this time. He had entered I-94 just as the gray Challenger zoomed by him. But it wasn't going too fast for Fahp's dash cam to record the vehicle. In the process, it also recorded at least 14 vehicles in various lanes. None of them was Arthur's car, but Fahp didn't notice that right away.

Exactly 17 seconds after the speeder passed Fahp, Mack passed by. So the speeder was well up the road. Lo and behold, four minutes later, Fahp sees Mack arresting Arthur beside his black, not gray, vehicle. Again, Fahp did not recall the color, thus the bad arrest, immediately.

Fahp, intending to commend good police work, posted the video online. (Here we go again … So, why is it that you guys don't realize that a), cameras are everywhere and b) there is something called the i-n-t-e-r-n-e-t?) But he soon got comments on the video from people who noticed the speeding car and the arrested man's car were not the same.

Fahp, clearly a citizen with a conscience, unlike the officer in this case, called the Allen Park Police Department. He talked directly to Mack, saying that the video showed Mack had stopped the wrong vehicle. Mack said he didn't want to see the video. Of course he didn't. He was too stupid to realize this was damning evidence whether he saw it or not, and should just cave in right away.

Well, Fahp isn't stupid. He posted the video on several other blogs. Not long after that, Mack's boss, Lieutenant Daniel Williams, got a call from an automotive journalist for a website who said there was this video online of the reckless driver and the arrest scene of the Wrong Guy. The journalist, Patrick George, said the owner of the video, Mr. Fahp, wanted to give the department the video to clear the poor guy who was falsely arrested.

Williams, to his credit, said he wanted to see the video and arranged to contact Fahp. The next day, Fahp came with the video.

It didn't take long for Mack to admit he was wrong. That was an understatement. The charges were dropped against Arthur, but the damage was done. The irony? If Mack had not lied, he would have had immunity, under the law we describe in Chapter Fourteen, for his "mistake."

Arthur suffered numbness and pain in his hands and fingers for days after the arrest; the pain continued even longer. Worse, though, is that Arthur suffered severe anxiety, depression and PTSD effects from the arrest, and sought treatment from a mental health counselor. It's not hard to understand why.

Meanwhile, in the days before the video was released that cleared Arthur, he had a duty to report his arrest to his employer because he had the CPL. His permit was suspended.

It would be nice to say this entire scenario of the bogus, ultimately violent traffic stop is rare. It is not.

On behalf of Arthur, I filed a lawsuit charging false arrest, assault and battery, intentional infliction of emotional distress and gross negligence.

There is plenty of case law that applies here. One statute offers immunity to cops like Mack if "the employee was acting, or reasonably believed he was acting, within the scope of his authority; the acts were undertaken in good faith, and the acts were discretionary, rather than ministerial, in nature."

Well, as we wrote in our brief, "a defendant is not acting in good faith when the governmental employee acts maliciously or with a wanton or reckless disregard of the rights of another..." Michigan law defines "wanton misconduct" as "conduct or a failure to act that shows such indifference to whether harm will result as to be equal to a willingness that harm will result."

Mack wasn't going to admit to lack of good faith. Officers rarely do. That's why courts review circumstantial evidence to determine motive in these cases.

For the reasons we've already listed, Mack had no basis for probable cause.

As for assault and battery, the definition of this is "any intentional unlawful offer of corporal injury to another person by force, or force unlawfully directed toward the person of another, under circumstances which create a well-founded apprehension of imminent contact, coupled with the apparent present ability to accomplish the contact."

A battery is "the willful and harmful or offensive touching of another person which results from an act intended to cause such contact."

To prove, in addition to this, "intentional infliction," we had to show "extreme and outrageous conduct; intent or recklessness; causation; and severe emotional distress." It was not hard to prove all of these conditions, as I'm sure you can see from our description of this incident.

False arrest was not difficult to depict here. Gross negligence is defined as "conduct so reckless as to demonstrate a substantial lack of concern for whether an injury results." We argued that even if Mack's treatment of Arthur were not intentional, it certainly was negligent. Just the false statements in Mack's report prove that.

Even so, the legal standard to prove this is physical injury, which certainly occurred.

Though this reads like an open-and-shut case, we have already explained in this book that there is no such thing. Still, my deposition of Mack should help seal the deal — for us. Mack tried to keep defending the idea that he could read that license plate clearly:

Q: Your observation at that time was that as the car was passing and you had gotten behind it, you observed the personalized plate, is that correct?

Mack: *Yes.*

Q: Okay. And that would have been an element, justification for probable cause, to believe that the car that you saw driving at 91 miles per hour was, in fact, the right car to arrest, correct?

Mack: *Yes.*

Moments later, Mack tried to testify that though he was facing west and Arthur was going east, he could read that personalized license plate:

Q: You've indicated that Mr. Chapman was not doing 91 miles an hour when he passed you, correct? The SHAKAZ plate was not doing 91 miles an hour?

Mack: *After this time period, after reviewing the videotape and having the time, no it was not.*

Q: Well, sir, you put in the report, you attribute the SHAKAZ plate as driving 91 miles an hour?

Mack: *Yes.*

Q: That's what you're leading people to believe in your report, correct?

Yes, Mack said, that's what he believed at the time of the report.

There isn't much more to say about this cop's flimsy, slimy behavior. As of this writing, this case was still in litigation.

But no matter how it resolves, nothing will erase the trauma of being so recklessly attacked out of absolutely nowhere as was Arthur. He still suffers from anxiety and PTSD.

CHAPTER SEVEN

Getting Away With Murder

I turn now to the 2006 case, *Arnetta Grable, Personal Representative of the Estate of Lamar Grable, Deceased v. Police Officer Eugene Brown.* This wrongful death case involved the shooting (eight times) of Lamar Grable by Officer Brown in 1996. Since Brown claimed Grable also shot him, twice, this proved to be one of my most challenging cases, but one in which we prevailed. This case involved a number of issues I already have raised here: the cop-as-hero syndrome; a misguided sense of probable cause; the abuse of use-of-force guidelines; the police code of silence; and the fallacy of the police-report-as-gospel.

Lamar Grable was, by all reports, a nice young man. Just 20 years old, he was raised in a nice, church-going extended family that included several police officers. Lamar, who was about 6 feet tall, around 170 pounds, grew up respecting these relatives and the rule of law. He also was an entrepreneur at an early age, owning several businesses.

On the night of Sept. 21, 1996, he was leaving a church dance in Detroit, where — it was key to learn later — all participants were searched for weapons before entering. Taking a shortcut across a vacant lot afterward to walk to his house, which was one block from the church, he was suddenly confronted by Detroit Police Officer Eugene Brown, a 6-foot-5-tall man with his gun drawn. Upon encountering Lamar, Brown shot him twice, and then another six times during and after Lamar fell to the ground.

It was essentially an execution. In Brown's report, he claimed to have been shot twice by Lamar Grable, which he repeated on the witness stand. He claimed he survived because he was wearing his bulletproof vest. This detail was important because it helped build around him the cop-as-hero aura, which certainly made very challenging the task of suing him for, it appeared, killing someone who was trying to kill him.

By 2000 or so, Lamar's poor mother, Arnetta, had already hired two lawyers to file a wrongful death civil suit against Brown and the DPD. Both conducted investigations and completed depositions with Brown and the officer who was his partner that night. Both tried to convince Arnetta to settle the case. She refused. She had lost her son, she knew it was a wrongful death and she wasn't going to settle, no-way, no-how. She wanted the truth. Who could blame her?

As a parent, I certainly understood her desire for justice. And here I was, a lawyer who had spent time as a cop, and then defending them. I saw in some cases various cover-up shenanigans, faulty or B.S. police reports among them. I had been behind the curtain, so to speak. So when Mrs. Grable was looking for another lawyer, I was the perfect fit. I told her, in fact, that I was probably the only lawyer who could win this case for her.

And once again, my college education played a role here. Since I majored in psychology, I had taken a child development course in which I learned about child-mother attachment, possibly the most powerful human connection. It's more than the *in utero* factor here. This attachment lasts until the end of life — the child's, hers or both. It's a bond that supersedes all others, and I had learned about that.

My own experience as a parent, and then representing other mothers, drove me to perform this service for this woman, to represent her in what all the other lawyers were telling me was a truly impossible case. I began my work with my able co-counsel Melissa El in 2001 — five years after this poor woman had lost her son.

Early on, of course, I read the etched-in-stone evidence: the police report. Heretofore, as a DPD lawyer, I had had to stick with the fiction in some of these reports. But now, I could read it and attack it. I could spot the B.S. and why it was written as it was. I also refused, once the trial began, to assume, or let the jury assume, that police reports are sacrosanct.

Here is the initial "Preliminary Complaint Record" Brown filed after the incident. I will not use standard abbreviations, i.e., "perp," which is "perpetrator," or "wrt," which means "writer," who was in this case Brown. I also will paragraph for easier reading and afterward point out what I immediately saw as the "B.S.," which stands for, well, you know.

During his "on duty patrol" that day, Brown wrote:

"On above day, date and time writer and partner were en route to Belle Isle, Harbormaster Section when writer, who was the passenger of scout car being driven by partner, westbound on St. Paul at E. Grand River Blvd., observed above-described perpetrator with a handgun in his hand then placing it in his pocket.

My partner and I then exited scout car and partner yelled to perpetrator to stop, police. Perpetrator then ran northbound across St. Paul and then northbound into the alley. Writer gave foot chase while partner returned to scout car. Approximately halfway down the alley perpetrator then ran eastbound between the houses, then northbound on Field (Street) for a couple houses, then eastbound between the houses.

"Partner in scout car followed perpetrator in driveway and perpetrator ran southbound to a vacant lot just north of the apartment building at 1764 Field. Writer ran eastbound into the vacant lot where writer observed perpetrator who was pointing (nickel-plated Revolver) at writer and perpetrator fired approximately two times at writer who in fear for his life returned fire two times at perpetrator from a distance of approximately five feet.

"Perpetrator then ran around a bush at the location, writer followed perpetrator who then turned around and ran directly at writer and at this point, writer and perpetrator collided and perpetrator again fired a couple more shots at writer.

"Writer, again in fear for his life, fired several more rounds at perpetrator from very close range, and perpetrator then fell to the ground. Scene was secured until responding units arrived moments later. Additional: Writer was struck with perpetrator's gunfire two times in abdomen."

I saw red flags immediately. First flag: It was obvious Brown didn't write the report. How did I know that so instantly and without question? Grammar. The report reads in the third and fourth paragraphs that Lamar "fired approximately two times at writer who in *fear for his life* returned fire two times at perpetrator from a distance of approximately five feet ... Writer, again *in fear for his life*, fired several more rounds ..." The use of the second-person pronoun "his" twice in this report, instead of the first-person pronoun "I," which is used elsewhere, signaled to me someone else wrote the report. That someone else just didn't catch this grammatical giveaway, but I did.

So, it was obvious the union lawyer wrote the report. This opened up all kinds of angles for my attack. First, the report was typed, versus handwritten. Brown's partner's report was handwritten, as most reports right after incidents were, at least back then. Also, this was a report about the most serious engagement of a police officer in the course of performing his duty: the use of deadly force. It would be the one used throughout anything that followed this incident.

How silly that the use of a particular word would clue me into the real story. Upon seeing that pronoun "his," I knew that report was only fodder for justifying Lamar's murder. And, more importantly, this meant that the person who wrote the report was *not a witness to the crim*e. I knew it had to have been the lawyer who at the very least dictated what Brown typed or typed it himself.

This was the biggest red flag to me. As a former DPD officer and lawyer, I also knew well that in shooting cases, many police departments have union lawyers ready to run to the rescue. This is their right, so police officers can — and often do — take all the time they need to tell their side of the story. They don't have to give their report immediately; they have union protection and can discuss the incident with the union lawyer before anyone, then or later, can get a fresh, unvarnished, un-lawyer-ized version of what happened. This report offered a propped-up version of the events in order to secure Brown's freedom. Thus, the late-breaking, doctored-up incident report becomes the etched-in-stone story that will last until the end of time.

But one often unasked question is: Does the department get the truth? *Does the department get the truth?* Who knows? But get this: The department still has the formal *obligation* to find the truth. Why was I the only one who saw that discrepancy in the report? It was reviewed by what is called the initial Board of Review, which police departments convene anytime there is a critical incident — part of that obligation to get at the truth. The Board consists of three executive officers, inspectors and other high-ranking department people. Their job in this case was to look at everything and determine whether or not the shooting of Lamar Grable was justified.

Their ruling? An overwhelming yes. It was justified. So they didn't see what I did in the report, or they just didn't care. Meanwhile, another red flag unrelated to the report arose when I learned Brown's partner was going to seek Fifth Amendment protection to avoid having to testify in the case.

Hmmm, I thought. Why? Taking the Fifth is a pretty serious, and always highly noticed, move by any potential witness. And yet, she wasn't even the shooter. Why was she taking the Fifth? Maybe ... to be able to avoid having to lie on the stand to protect her partner? Huge red flag. It was a red flag to others, apparently, including the media, which was making inquiries. This scrutiny and just the oddity of Brown's partner taking the Fifth resulted in Detroit Police Chief Benny Napoleon convening what is called a "Super Board of Review" to reinvestigate whether Lamar Grable's shooting was justified.

We tried legally to get those reports and any other materials by entering that public records boxing ring I mentioned earlier, to try to penetrate that hardcore reluctance of police departments to release anything to the public, even if it furthers justice. Clearly the public had a right to know how Lamar died. It didn't matter. We never got to see those reports. The scant information we had available was what had been gathered in prior investigations from the lawyers who Mrs. Grable had hired before. It wasn't much. That included forensics evidence, or the lack thereof. We had no idea. But we knew that Lamar had been shot at point-blank range as he lay on the ground. That meant bullets should have been found there. None were found. You can make your own assumptions about what happened to them.

We were shut out on much of this because when we took this case, the judge told us we had to take it "as is," mainly because the case had been in the system for five years. It was like buying a used car. We could not conduct any discovery in an "as-is" case, either. We did what we could, and made progress. We hired a consulting expert for the ballistics, Dave Balash. Dr. Werner Spitz was our forensic pathologist. I knew Spitz would testify that Lamar had to have been on the ground when these contact shots were fired. The reason was that if Lamar were shot in the front against a solid surface, the ground, it would alter the pattern of the entrance and exit wounds. And in fact, Lamar had exit wounds that appeared to be entrance wounds. It was a technical item, but a very important one. This kind of evidence would show the shooting was indeed execution-style.

One contact wound described in the original autopsy was an entry wound to Grable's left rear arm. The autopsy clearly described this bullet wound on Grable's skin in the shape of the barrel of Brown's gun. Neither the Board of Review, nor Brown in any of his reports or versions of the shooting, accounted for this wound. It was a gratuitous shot by Brown that evidenced his diabolical, murderous intent. It was the type of shot that could not have occurred in any struggle, and Brown never could offer an explanation for that type of shot. It was just more proof that supported expert testimony that the shots Brown offered were execution style.

We also learned that Brown was trigger-happy. In six years with the department, he had shot at nine people, killing three. That's more than a red flag, it's a neon sign. And — here we go again — Board of Review reports had been completed for each shooting. But the Board for our case never looked at these prior reports. Supposedly, each report is independent, and that's to protect the officer. But the number of shootings alone by Brown should have rendered him unfit to be on the street. Those were the tools I had as we prepared to go to trial. We had to mostly rely on our own experience, expertise, determination and just plain daring.

CHAPTER EIGHT

The Hot Dog Syndrome

W hat goes on in a courtroom is often a crapshoot. While I knew what I had and where I would be going with witnesses, especially Officer Brown, I knew that nothing was guaranteed. A strong defense by the DPD lawyers; the judge's ruling that I take the case "as is"; a mis-speak by one of my witnesses; a juror who sounded good but turned out to be shaky — any of these could sink the ship.

And while we knew about the nine shootings and three deaths, the jury did not.

Add to that a wagon load of other lawyers telling me I was nuts for taking this case: "He shot a cop, man."

But something about this case resonated with me, touched my heart in the deepest sense. It connected me emotionally to my own mother, to whom I was so close and who had been such a strong influence and role model. While it was a seemingly impossible fight, I knew it was one that my mother, like Arnetta, would not have abandoned.

The trial took place in July and August of 2006 in Wayne County Circuit Court in Detroit. Over the course of the proceedings, I worked to disassemble Brown's defense one piece at a time. First, I hammered the fact that Brown, throughout this dramatic, so-called life-threatening scenario, never stopped to radio for help.

As I said earlier in this book, that is perhaps the first and most important step officers can take to ensure their safety and that of the citizens they interact with. I began:

Q: "When you reported to work that day, you were provided with a prep radio, right?" (A prep radio is what the officers use to broadcast to those outside the scout car.)

Brown: "Yes, I was."

Q: "... The prep radio is designed to contact your Dispatcher for various purposes, correct?"

Brown: "Correct."

Q: "It is designed to call for help, is it not? If you need it?"

Brown: "If I need it, yes."

Q: "You also have what I believe is something called an auto vehicle locator in the car, correct? ... And that's a button that you use for emergencies, correct?"

Brown: "As a last resort, yes, sir."

Q: "As a last resort if you don't know where you're at? And you're in trouble?"

Brown: "As a last resort when you can't communicate on the radio."

Q: "You didn't communicate on that radio that day, did you?"

Brown: "No, I did not."

A little later in the cross examination, I also reviewed with Brown that he was in uniform, in a clearly marked police car, headlights on. There was no mistaking who and what was on hand to any citizen in the area.

Once he had spotted the man he claimed later was Lamar, he said he saw a gun in Lamar's hand. He saw him switch the gun from one hand to another, and then attempt to conceal the gun as Brown approached him. I continued:

Q: "Now, you see a guy with a gun, it's dark outside, you have a gun, you've got a radio. You've got an emergency button, you've got a prep radio, and I believe you say that he sees you and then he cuts in front of your car, correct? ... Your partner, I think, is driving and she stops the car, correct?"

Brown: "Yes, she does."

Q: "Okay. You don't call to Dispatch at that point in time to tell the

Dispatch, 'Dispatch, this is ... B.I. 2 (referring to Belle Isle), we are located at St. Paul and E. Grand Boulevard, we got a man with a gun and he's switching it from hand to hand, now he's put it in his waistband,' or whatever, did you?"

Brown: *"No, sir."*

Q: *"Okay. There wouldn't have been anything wrong with doing that, would it have?"*

Brown: *"I didn't have time to do that, sir."*

Q: *"You didn't? You were inside the car, you saw the guy with the gun, you were in a protective environment so to speak inside the police car and you got the radio. How far is that from you?"*

Brown: *"About a half a foot."*

Q: *"How long does it take you to grab the radio ... How long does that take you?"*

Brown: *"Same time for that subject to disappear if I didn't chase him."*

Q: *"Did he disappear, sir, from the time that you first saw him to the time that you and your partner got out of the car and you began to chase him? Did he disappear?"*

Brown: *"He attempted to, sir, yes."*

Nice try. But it was clear to the jury at this point that Brown was going solo, against all the training, ethical procedures and just plain common sense. He was being stupid.

I also pointed out Brown could have called for the police helicopter, which had spotlights that would have illuminated the entire area, and reduced any danger that Brown would be shot by a man he couldn't see.

I carefully constructed alternative scenes, each that would have eliminated any need to use deadly force. Instead, as I pointed out, Brown was, I believe, falling victim to that hero burden — that because we always believe cops are heroes, they feel they have to act like one. And heroes tend not to ask for help.

Remember the police department provision: "An imminent threat is the perception of danger from any action or outcome that may occur during an encounter *absent any such action by law enforcement.*" I add that for emphasis and to bring up again the dynamic of hero officers creating danger.

That means that when Brown was being a hero, going in and out of dark places looking for the man with a gun, who was a danger to him — and meanwhile not taking one step to get help — he created his own danger. Then he attempted to justify his use of deadly force against the danger he created.

That's what all these police officers do. In every one of those national cases, as well as those I present in this book, it's always the danger they create themselves, and then react to "in fear of their lives." This isn't a hero syndrome; it's the hot dog syndrome. These guys are just hot dogs trying to be cool.

Brown: *"I didn't have to call, sir."*

Q: *"Cause you didn't want to call because you could handle it yourself. You could handle this man with a gun by yourself, couldn't you?"*

Brown: *"I've done it many times before, wrestled a person with a gun."*

He would have been embarrassed, laughed at, I suggested, by his fellow hero-officers. It was ego, I argued. Had he called for assistance, which he admitted would have come, "perhaps there would have been a different outcome, Mr. Brown. Perhaps it would not have resulted in someone's death."

It is so important, it must be repeated. Brown and Grable both should have gone home safe that night. Even if Lamar had had a gun, that has to be the goal of law enforcement. It goes back to the Code of Ethics. Lamar Grable is who these ethics refer to. So are Tamir Rice, Eric Garner — all of them are whom the Code was designed to protect. If you read the provisions of any deadly force policy, it tells the officer what he *can't* do. They warn him of the multifaceted tragedy of taking a life.

Brown didn't listen.

CHAPTER NINE

Unraveling the Fallacy

A fter establishing that Officer Brown failed to call for help, thus creating danger, I attacked the ghostwritten report issue. This is how that exchange went, beginning with my initial question on the subject:

Q: *"I'm going to hand you what's been marked as Plaintiff's exhibit No. 1 and ask whether or not you can identify that. It's a report that you prepared concerning this ... incident that had your signature on it."*

Brown: *"Yes, it is."*

Q: *"... Now again, Mr. Brown, that's a report that is dated 9-21-96 and that was the date of this incident, correct?"*

Brown: *"That's correct."*

Q: *"It is a report that is entitled 'Shots Fired by Police Officer,' correct?"*

Brown: *"That's correct."*

Q: *"It has your signature on it, correct?"*

Brown: *"Yes, it does."*

Q: *"It has a date of 9-21-96, but that's not when this Report was prepared, correct?"*

Brown: *"That's correct."*

Q: *"The Report was prepared two days later, correct ... The Report was prepared by your lawyer at the time, correct?"*

Brown: *"Yes."*

Q: *"Your Union lawyer at the time, not by you?"*

Brown: *"I was there. I'm the one that dictated it to him, sir."*

Q: *"And you didn't type it, right?"*

Brown: *"No, sir, I did not."*

Q: *"You conferred with the lawyer prior to this report being typed by the lawyer, correct?"*

Brown: *"That's our policy, yes, sir."*

Q: *"And that's the Detroit Police Department Policy, to sit down and discuss the facts of the case with the lawyer and have the lawyer type the report up, is that correct?"*

Brown: *"No, sir, it's for our lawyer to represent us when we're making a report. I couldn't type the report."*

Q: *"I'm talking about procedure because you just said that's the way the things operate in the Detroit Police Department. You get into a shooting, you shoot somebody, the persons who are in charge of the investigation don't get to talk to you about the shooting until you sit down with the lawyer who represents the Union and the Police Officers and you discuss the whole case with him, he types it up. Then you turn the report in two days later and you put the date of the incident on the report. Is that —"*

Brown: *"Sir, I couldn't do the report on the night of the incident. I was shot and in the hospital Emergency Room at (Detroit) Receiving (Hospital)."*

Again, nice try. Here, Brown was trying to squeeze even more sympathetic tears from the jury as the "poor-me" officer who had to murder someone because he was not only in fear of his life, but he was shot at by said vicious criminal. I didn't let this stop me.

Q: *"Sir, you didn't type this report up. You could talk even though you claim you were shot, correct?"*

Brown: *"I was in the Emergency Room at Receiving, sir."*

Brown tried to imply he was there all night. I stopped that fallacy, too.

Q: *"…You weren't in the hospital all night, you were in there for a number of hours, correct?"*

Brown: *"Correct."*

Q: "*So, you wait two days to meet with the lawyer to discuss with the lawyer what the case was about, the facts, what you did, or claimed. He types the report up, you weren't prohibited from talking after you got out of the hospital. You didn't type the report up, so there was nothing that would have prevented you from talking to whomever after you got out of the hospital, but you wait two days, correct?*"

Brown tried to fudge that timeline, but essentially, he had to own up to the point I was making — that the report was done well after the fact, and with a lot of legal, Union-inspired help. As in, fiction. Score one for the plaintiff.

Next, I took Brown through the winding, chaotic chase through vacant lots, behind houses, in a field and by that church where Lamar had been to the dance. I specifically highlighted that Brown and his partner lost sight of the man with the weapon more than once. This helped reinforce the idea that in the dark, they could have been chasing two completely different men. I was also building in the mind of the jury that they were creating danger.

In other words, I was suggesting that Brown chased, and ultimately killed, the wrong guy.

After pointing out major inconsistencies in the supposed distance between Brown and Lamar that Brown listed in reports (30 feet versus 5 feet, a glaring discrepancy), I went meticulously over Brown's version of what happened once he and Lamar encountered one another.

Brown said Lamar raised his gun at him and shot at him twice, missing. Brown shot back immediately, he said, and did not miss. "I was defending my life. As soon as he shot at me I shot at him." There it is, the perennial explanation: *I was in fear for my life.*

Lamar miraculously managed to get up and run away while still shooting at Brown, according to Brown. He ran behind a large mound of dirt and trees, blocking Brown's view of him. He stopped and, Brown said, "waited for me to come around the mound." He also checked the nearby alley to see if Lamar had fled that way. Brown was still running when, he said, "I saw the subject running up towards me ... The gentleman ran right up to me with the gun."

Lamar supposedly raised his gun with his right hand. Brown said he put his left arm over Lamar's and pushed the weapon down. "I told him to drop the weapon ... He fired two shots."

Thus, Brown sustained two shots to his midsection, but he shot back four times. And Lamar "went down at that point." But Lamar appeared to be raising his gun again, he added.

Brown shot Lamar again, four times, at point-blank range. I raised evidence that if this were true, the bullets should have gone through Lamar's body and been found in the ground. But none were found.

And even more damning, the gun found at the scene was what cops call "a throwaway gun," or a gun cops keep to plant by victims they have killed unjustifiably. Equally important, Lamar's prints were not found on the gun; there was no DNA evidence linking that gun to Lamar.

I presented evidence that the bullet holes in Brown's shirt also contradicted his description of how Lamar supposedly shot him as the two collided. The ultimate theory that I proposed, and that the jury apparently believed, was that Brown, after executing an innocent kid who had no gun, shot himself — carefully— to cover for what had happened.

Related to this, and perhaps the lynchpin of my entire case came when I got Brown to admit he "may" have carried out an execution.

I call this, with all due humility, my "Perry Mason moment." I knew I was taking a huge risk to ask this next question. I knew, if it backfired, it could undermine the substantial progress we had made against Brown. But that progress was solid evidence.

As I considered this next question, I went with my gut. I knew the details of this case and this guy. I had watched him, listened to him. I'm looking at him, thinking, this guy is nuts. So I'm going to ask.

Q: *"Mr. Grable was on the ground over here and you fire those four shots, you know now, into his chest, point-blank range, contact range, as he fell to the ground. Let me ask you this. Is it possible, sir, that rather than Mr. Grable being erect, that he was instead already down on the ground and you punitively, kneeling down on one knee, sir, pumping him with those four rounds? Is that possible?"*

Amazingly, Brown answered: *"That's possible."*

I could barely believe what I was hearing. I imagine Brown's counsel felt the same way. I honestly wonder if this stupid guy himself even understood what he had just done. From that moment, it was case closed. (This particular exchange later was used in the Court of Appeals ruling that denied Brown's request for appeal.)

Keep in mind here: This all took place before cell phones, dashboard videos — all the tools that are helping to nail the cops doing these things today. I had to prove this case from scratch, without all of the evidence that we weren't allowed to use via this "as-is" case.

It boiled down to Brown's word against a dead man, and dead men don't talk. It was an impossible case — unless you knew where to look, how to recreate the fallacy, the fiction that usually works like a charm to get judges and juries to go along with the mantras and the cover stories.

The jury found Brown guilty of gross negligence and assault and battery. They awarded Arnetta Grable $4 million. It was a good day, but nothing could ever make up for the loss of her son, another casualty of a cop culture that too often enables cops not just to commit murder, but to be their own worst enemies.

This case, I repeat, illustrates all that can, and often does, go wrong in the cases we are seeing on the news so often today.

Had Brown followed the suggested steps, starting with radioing for backup, and followed the DPD's rules governing officers' use of firearms, had he not felt the pressure to be a hero, Lamar would not have been killed.

But Brown went solo, and Lamar died. Brown returned to duty. He lived to kill another day. Arnetta passed away in 2018.

CHAPTER TEN

When the Good Guy is Bad

I have talked about how a person's human frailties or traits do not disappear when that person becomes a police officer. Those traits, in fact, are nurtured, in a sense, and often become worse as cops perform their duty.

I've described how the nature of the job itself creates so many situations that a susceptible cop can play right into. The thief robs, the liar lies and so forth. That is the crux of the human animal.

Perhaps the worst example of this character flaw made powerful via the police uniform is sexual deviancy.

Let's start with an example.

I was hired to handle the case of Tiffany Dixon. She sued the City of Detroit under 42 U.S.C. §1983, a key civil rights statute which we explain in detail in Chapter Twelve.

This is what happened.

Dixon called 911 one evening because her boyfriend, who lived with her, was angry and destroying property. He was not beating her, but who knows if it might have come to that. In any case, she called 911 over and over again, saying, "He's back, he's back."

Detroit Police Officer Deon Nunlee finally showed up with his partner at about 3 a.m. Naturally, Dixon was dressed like it's nighttime; she was wearing bed clothes, with no bra, and perhaps was missing a button or two. It didn't take long after the boyfriend settled down and just went to bed for Nunlee to order Dixon upstairs while his knowing partner guarded the door.

Nunlee was upstairs for a long time, having his way with her. He forced her to touch his penis while he touched her breasts and vagina. Then he raped her. He did this *twice*, and then — you can't make this up — *he got her phone number*, telling her he would call the next morning, so he could "fuck the shit out of her." As if she had enjoyed getting raped by him.

Think about the psychology here; he's thinking what he did is not a crime and that she was a willing participant. He's so full of himself, he's going to call her back the next day. He interprets his conduct as mutual consent and not extortive. Of course, he committed a heinous crime that will scar his victim for the rest of her life. A robber does not get his victim's phone number and promise to call back the next day to re-rob that victim.

Nunlee was so comfortable in his criminal commission that he did, in fact, call Dixon the next morning. This was the psychological underpinning wrapped in his police mind, that even in full uniform on duty, he is somehow performing a public service for this vulnerable citizen — that he handled her emergency. It bears noting that his run sheet reflected all he had done to assist her, except the sexual assault.

So again, Nunlee doesn't think he committed a crime, despite common decency. This proclivity is typical of how many police officers get into these sexual deviancies. It's all part of the police subculture, the relationship of power. He's got a gun, right? She sees the gun, and if she resists, it's, "I can arrest you if you don't do what I ask." It becomes extortion.

The next morning, Dixon did not answer Nunlee's call. What a shock — to him, maybe. Instead, Dixon called a friend for help and the case eventually made its way to police department Internal Affairs.

This is just one example of many — more than you can imagine. Sexually deviant cops have, and take advantage of, all kinds of "opportunities" on the job. Imagine the young woman who runs a light late in the evening and doesn't want to get an expensive ticket. The cop gives her a choice. Same thing with women pulled over for drunk driving, and on and on it goes.

It all goes back to what I said: If you are a pervert before becoming a cop, you don't change, and arguably get worse, because these opportunities present themselves, for a multitude of reasons. Chief among them is the refusal of police departments to admit the problem, that this deviancy is so generic to the job hazard, a result of the police head-in-the-sand attitude, which thus becomes the rationalization that this is just one man, one case, i.e., it's only Nunlee's fault. He should have known better.

The sheer frequency in which these on-duty rapes occur make it a department-wide problem, not just the offending cop's problem.

For the individual pervert cop, it's back to power and the perception that the public has of police officers, and how male police officers see themselves in relationship to females. Somehow that uniform and position of power make a cop more attractive to women — but so often *in his own brain*. I labor to emphasize that point.

A police officer might perceive any woman that he stops as falling all over him — absurd, you think, but not to him because that perception is in his brain. The occasion for opportunities don't help, though that is no excuse for criminal sexual assault.

When I was in uniform, it seemed true that the man — and these days woman, too — in uniform is always attractive. When I was working, a lot of women wanted to flirt with me. Problem is, when the officer takes the uniform off, that same perception is still there — in his mind.

So instead of politely warding off the flirting, the deviant cop takes advantage of the situation. This happens often, in every police department. But the culture, the cop-is-hero and all the other stuff we've described in this book, allows the perversion to continue largely unabated. That only reinforces the cop's perception that he's not doing anything wrong.

A prime example is the case of David Witherspoon. While it was litigated in 2002, the cited abuses happened throughout the 1990s — and that tells you that there were abuses well before that, throughout Witherspoon's career. One of the plaintiffs in this case was Denise Diamond.

On Labor Day in 1999, Diamond was driving to work in Detroit when Witherspoon, a Detroit Police sergeant, pulled her over. He was working his normal midnight shift, optimal for his deceptive behavior: fewer witnesses. Limited illumination. Other supervisors "in the hole" — code for when cops go to take a nap on duty.

Diamond ran a yellow light, no big deal. At least not until Witherspoon got involved. He asked her for identification, went back to his car, then called for her via his loudspeaker. So this was already jarring for Diamond. Witherspoon told her that she had two warrants out for her arrest; these were likely traffic tickets, nothing serious, but Diamond didn't know that. She only heard a threat and saw his gun.

He then said, "I can either take you to jail, or we can make some type of arrangements."

"I'm going to work," Diamond told him. He suggested that they just go around the corner to do the deed. He talked about how freaky he was and how he liked threesomes. Diamond, feeling panic at this point, said she had to go to work, that she couldn't be late, either. Witherspoon offered to write a note for her. Diamond still said, "No." Witherspoon then bragged about how big his penis was and unzipped his pants to display it. He told her to "rub it." Diamond felt trapped and complied.

But that wasn't enough for Witherspoon. He told Diamond to expose her breasts and then her butt so he could photograph them. Again, she complied, as she did when he told her to put her mouth on his penis. He finally let her go — and, like Nunlee in our previous example, gave his victim his phone number. So here we have another cop who thinks he is performing a public service, and that his reward is her "consensual" concession.

The sick irony in these cases is that the guy who is supposed to catch the crook is the crook.

But wait, it gets better.

Witherspoon referred to himself on this, and all the other times he did such things to women, as "Deon." So the guy's got an alias? Yet, think about it: His real name is right on his uniform. And yet he adopts this pseudonym. This is either a pseudonym for his sexual prowess in his own mind, or a futile attempt to hide his deviant behavior in plain sight.

In any case, Diamond told her co-workers what had happened, and she later told her sister, Vanessa. And guess what? Turns out a few days before "Deon" assaulted Diamond, he had done the same thing to Vanessa!

Diamond suffered emotional damage, as you might imagine. She remains terrified of being stopped by police, sought counseling and quit her job because she knew that "Deon" was still out there pa-"trolling."

Witherspoon got away with this and many other assaults until another victim, Toyia Moody, blew the whistle on him. She, the Diamond sisters and still another victim named Stephanie Bennett were interviewed by Internal Affairs.

Eventually, these victims sued Witherspoon and the City of Detroit under the Elliott-Larsen Civil Rights Act and 42 U.S.C §1983. The landmark Elliott-Larsen Michigan law guarantees citizens protection from discrimination based on a person's sex or membership in a certain class and aims to eliminate the effects of offensive or demeaning stereotypes, prejudices and biases.

Specifically, we charged Witherspoon with negligence in operation of a motor vehicle; intentional infliction of emotional distress; assault and battery; violation of public accommodation of public service; and civil rights violations.

Discovery in the lawsuit turned up a horrendous path of destruction by Witherspoon. He and his partner sexually harassed a woman working at a shoe store, for example. He also sexually harassed his fellow female police officers. His accusers — Diamond, along with her sister, Bennett and Moody — suffered the more personal trauma. Moody and Bennett were sexually assaulted, battered and photographed.

When forced to face his crimes during the lawsuit, Witherspoon had to acknowledge he had stopped many women as he had Diamond, but refused to own up to more than 30 such incidents.

Are you believing this? "Yeah, I did it, but, hey, not more than 30 times. Honest."

Not only that, but it stands to reason other cops saw this and knew all about it. According to his later testimony, Witherspoon bragged to them about all of these crimes. That none of his fellow officers thought to report him again indicates the scope of the problem.

And on it goes — endlessly, it seems. To be sure you understand how bad it is, I refer to a 2008 *Law Journal* article that details dozens of police misconduct cases dealing with sexual deviancy and assaults. I cannot begin to summarize all of it; this is a 6,300-word article. The article was cited by Americans for Effective Law Enforcement (AELE), which describes itself as "a research-driven educational organization that produces and disseminates legal information through traditional seminars, via electronic media and direct contact."

It bears mentioning here that I serve on the board of another watchdog organization, the National Police Accountability Project, which also seeks to shine a light on these abuses in the hope of eventually eradicating them.

Our case against Witherspoon was among those listed in this article. A few other examples:

"A county sheriff hired a deputy, who was allegedly provided with little or no training. The deputy was first assigned duties as a jailer, and later, as a 'road deputy.' During his last week on the job, after resigning to pursue a position with the state Department of Corrections, he encountered a female employee at a convenience store who asked his advice on some legal problems. She declined his offer to go on a date with him. Learning that she had several outstanding arrest warrants, and owed approximately $800 in fees and fines, he drove to the store on his last day on the job, arrested her and transported her to the jail, telling her that he would not have done so if she had agreed to the date. At the jail, the deputy bet a jailer that he could get the arrestee to reveal her breasts. He then told the arrestee that he could get her fines reduced if she would show him her breasts, and she eventually complied. He then allegedly grabbed her exposed breast. She sued the deputy and the sheriff, claiming that the sheriff failed to properly train the deputy. The deputy was also arrested and pled guilty to second-degree sexual assault. The deputy had received a policy manual, but had not been required to read it, and, in fact, did not read it. He was scheduled to attend a training academy but had not yet attended it at

the time of the incident. The trial court found the deputy liable, as well as the sheriff in his official capacity, while granting the sheriff qualified immunity in his individual capacity. A federal appeals court overturned the inadequate training liability, noting that there was no duty specified in state statutes for sheriffs to train subordinates not to sexually assault detainees, and that there had been no past pattern of such conduct by the sheriff's deputies that would have put him on notice about the need for such training. Additionally, since a reasonable officer would know that intentionally sexually assaulting a detainee was illegal, and the deputy admitted that he knew 'that such conduct was impermissible,' the plaintiff failed to show that the lack of training caused the assault. *Parrish v. Ball*, #08-3517, 2010 U.S. App. Lexis 2748 (8th Cir.)."

"A woman who claimed that she was sexually assaulted by a former police officer claimed that her rape was the result of the police chief's failure to adequately supervise the officer. A federal appeals court found that summary judgment for the police chief and city were proper because there was insufficient evidence that the police chief acted with deliberate indifference. While the chief knew of four prior excessive force and unlawful arrest allegations against the officer, all arising from the same incident, prior to the alleged rape, there were no accusations that the officer engaged in sexual misconduct. In the absence of a pattern of similar incidents involving sexual misconduct, the plaintiff could not establish deliberate indifference as required for a failure to supervise claim. The appeals court did, however, uphold a jury's award of $50,000 in compensatory and $250,000 in punitive damages against the former officer, and rejected arguments that the punitive damage award was excessive. *Lewis v. Pugh*, No. 07-40662, 2008 U.S. App. Lexis 17748 (Unpub. 5th Cir.)."

"Federal appeals court reverses trial judge's grant of summary judgment to city in lawsuit brought by female motorist who claimed that police officer broke into her home and sexually assaulted her after obtaining her home address from her driver's license during traffic stop *which might have been aimed solely at finding out where she lived. Court speculates that Illinois Supreme Court might find that the officer, because of his assertion of his official authority, acted within the scope of his employment, triggering a duty, on the part of the city, to indemnify the officer for any judgment against him. Doe v. City of Chicago, No. 03-2221, 2004 U.S. App. Lexis 3811 (7th Cir. 2004). [2004 LR Apr]"*

"County and sheriff were not liable, under either Ohio state law or federal civil rights law, for a deputy's sexual advances made towards a minor girl while off duty, even though he was in uniform and using a county-owned van to transport his daughter and her friends home from a movie. Deputy acted outside of the scope of his employment and did not act 'under color' of law. Ramey v. Mudd, No. 02CA14, 798 N.E.2d 57 (Ohio App. 2003). [2004 LR Feb]"

Linked to this sexual deviancy reality is why Diamond, her sister, or many other women assaulted like this fail to report these assaults immediately — or at all.

The literature in the field also speaks to this phenomenon. One study, "Addressing Sexual Offenses and Misconduct by Law Enforcement," published by the International Association of Chiefs of Police, states:

"Victims may be reluctant to report an incident and/or participate in the investigation for a variety of reasons, including trauma of the incident; fear of not being believed; retaliation from the perpetrator or other officers; and previous bad experiences with law enforcement. These same reasons may account for why a victim recants or seeks to withdraw a complaint. A victim's reluctance to participate in an investigation is neither indicative of a false allegation nor reason to forego a thorough investigation. A detailed investigation should uncover unethical or illegal conduct just as it will reveal unfounded claims."

Witherspoon was convicted. When Internal Affairs searched his locker, there were about 100 photographs in his locker of different nude women he had assaulted. Did you get that? He had 100 photos *in his police locker* of naked women he had assaulted. You know other cops had to have seen this.

This dovetails into my point that police departments just blame the individual cop, which avoids the impact of the numbers, of how these repeated actions by deviant police officers is the symptom of a greater disease. And it isn't just sexual assault. In fact, assault is merely a subset of a broader deviancy that encompasses assault, harassment and less explicit sexual misbehaviors throughout police culture. The literature we cite here bears testimony to that.

The case of former Detroit Police Chief Ralph Godbee is a good example. His behavior fell into this broader spectrum of sexual deviancy. And as the CEO, if you will, of this public corporation, his examples should set the highest standard of behavior. If the CEO is cavorting and picking and choosing among the sea of female subordinates, it can only signal approval of such behavior.

In 2012, then-Detroit Mayor Dave Bing suspended Godbee after Officer Angelica Robinson, working in Internal Affairs, revealed the two had been having an affair; Godbee was married at the time. So was Robinson.

But Robinson wanted to end this relationship. Godbee didn't like that. He wanted Robinson where he wanted her, despite the fact that he a) was still married and b) was fooling around with other women as well. This became apparent when he went to a police conference in California with another woman.

Robinson, upset he was with this other woman, posted a photo on Twitter showing her with her gun in her mouth.

Godbee's response? He had his fellow officers put Robinson under surveillance. And I doubt it was genuine concern, but him trying to control the situation. He was on the phone to Internal Affairs as this was going on. He was trying to get some of the officers to intercept her, not for her safety, but so he wouldn't have to deal with the consequences of a potentially tragic situation.

So if you're wondering why sexual deviancy goes on unabated from police headquarters to the patrol car and private homes, consider the tone set with Godbee. The guy is the *Chief of Police*. A police department takes on the personality of the chief, essentially. And those working for him or her take their cues. There was nothing overtly illegal that Godbee did, which tells you he didn't recognize the scope of the problem of sexual deviancy. He probably didn't recognize it at all.

So if the Police Chief is having all these relationships with police women, including married women, trolling the department like it was his choice, personal harem, what does that tell the troops — and those susceptible to this hazard of the job?

I'd like to call all of this a soap opera, but it's too tragic to reduce it to that.

To be fair, the problem has been addressed in a few corners. Along with the above-cited police chief association excerpt is a study called "To Serve and Pursue: Exploring Police Sexual Violence Against Women" by Peter B. Kraska and Victor E. Kappeler of Eastern Kentucky University. This study appeared in the book *From Police and Society: Touchstone Readings, Second Edition*, and "identifies and examines an unexplored criminological phenomenon, termed here police sexual violence."

The study details that:

"...The police literature that alludes to PSV (police sexual violence) addresses the phenomenon as 'police sexual misconduct,' emphasizing the on-duty 'consensual sex' activities of a male officer with a female citizen...

"The police officer comes into contact with a number of females during his routine patrol duties. These contacts occur under conditions which provide numerous opportunities for illicit sex ... The officer also has the opportunity to stop a number of women coming home after a night of drinking. An intoxicated female may decide that her sexual favors are a small price to pay in order to avoid arrest of driving while intoxicated ... The woman may also be coerced into the act by a 'rogue' officer, but on numerous occasions the woman is more than ... willing... There are also a number of women who are attracted to the uniform or the aura of the occupation.

"... This 'consensual sex' assumption inhibits alternative, more victim-

based conceptualizations of police sexual violence. The view of this phenomenon as a problem of sexual favors assumes tacitly that deviant police are passive actors who are 'corrupted,' rather than active 'corruptors.'

"More important, it undermines the recognition of police sexual deviance as violent crime committed against women by relegating it to 'sexual favors,' as a result, the coercive nature of these encounters is masked. This assumption of consensual sex also reinforces the untested notion that the rogue, aberrant officer would use direct coercion, force or the authority of the badge in such encounters. Collectively, this thinking promotes a lack of serious attention to the phenomenon, promotes a conceptualization of police sexual deviance that denies the violence associated with sexual victimization and negates the possibility of a systematic or occupationally generated form of police victimization of women."

Research and studies notwithstanding, this sickness continues because too many departments refuse to admit it's a problem. That's why it never stops — and it won't, unless measures are taken.

For instance, cops need to be formally educated that they will be encountering these temptations on the job and be cognizant of their susceptibility to them. Then, when they find themselves in those situations, maybe a bell will go off.

Another effective tactic would be constant monitoring by supervisors of subordinate officers, looking for signs in these domestic calls. Perhaps the supervisor can even join the officer making that run, to be certain the victim is protected.

Another suggestion is that the department should visibly react to these situations. For instance, when a cop is shot in the line of duty, the department inevitably holds a debriefing in which they strategize how to avoid future attacks on cops. Why, then, can't they react in the same way when the cop is the perpetrator in order to avoid future harm to citizens?

It isn't enough to assume a cop who has been trained to understand the elements of the crime should know better. And at present, that is the only response of the department: "You should know better." Instead, the focus should shift to protecting the interest of citizens, just as police departments focus on protecting police officers after an officer is injured or killed.

I hope those involved in this police culture will begin to see this widespread dysfunction.

CHAPTER ELEVEN

Death by Jailer

S o far, we have addressed many issues on the subject of police misconduct. We've discussed probable cause, excessive force, unjustified use of deadly force, sexual assault and much more. Now we come to the next step in the law enforcement process: what happens after you are arrested. Once a person is arrested, they are taken into custody, usually at the local police department or county jail. These people are referred to as "pre-trial jail detainees" and remain so unless they are eventually found guilty in a court of law. If so, they become either "prisoners" or "inmates."

Now, that period of time between arrest and when a person is found innocent or guilty can be days, weeks or months. And it is just too easy, I have found, for those in charge of overseeing jail detainees — we will call them "jailers" — to forget the "presumed innocent" reality. And that can lead to very ugly, even deadly, consequences for jail detainees, whether or not they are guilty of their alleged crimes.

As my law practice delved further into this area, the phrase "jail death" became all too common. So it was that preventing jail deaths became one of my major campaigns. As it turned out, my cases helped lead to major reform. As I said, jail detainees linger behind bars for long periods of time while the wheels of justice, or injustice, grind into action — or linger in inaction. During this period, illnesses the jail detainee could freely seek help for outside of a cell instead fall into the discretionary hands of the jailer to treat.

So jail detainees are at the mercy, or too often the lack thereof, of the people who are supposedly in charge of their well-being. It is key to recognize one fact: The jailer comes into play after the arresting officer turns the care of the arrestee over to them. He is far from the scene of the arrest and never even reads the arrest report. Rarely will he even speak to the arresting officer. The detention officer processes the arrestee by fingerprinting him, photographing him, confirming his identity and reporting any injuries or health-related complaints the now-jail detainee may have.

In theory at least, the jailer should have no beef with the jail detainee because he resisted arrest or would not immediately comply with the arresting officer. Conclusion: *The jailer has absolutely no motive to harm jail detainees, right?* If only that were so.

The deplorable, medieval attitudes that I witnessed in a series of pre-trial jail detainee cases in the Detroit Police Department and in Wayne County were, in my experience, a new kind of misconduct that elevates to the status of evil. The U.S. Department of Justice eventually compelled change, but that was still in the future when I handled my first jail death cases.

Let's begin with Larry Bell. Larry was arrested for a probation violation in October 1997. He was in his early 40s and was addicted to heroin, so he was sick, whether we like to apply that term or not. At the time, police departments were not required to do basic medical histories of people coming into custody. That meant people with drug addiction, chronic obstructive pulmonary disease, heart attacks — whatever, it didn't matter. You were on your own if you were in jail.

There *was* a written policy that required monitoring of someone undergoing withdrawal. The policy required lifesaving action *must* be taken upon observation of serious signs of illness. Throwing up, sweating profusely, shaking like an epileptic, spitting up blood, cramping and smelling of a foul odor were signs of illness, as in withdrawal, in a heroin addict. It is not hard to figure this out. But these symptoms were,

I learned, simply not serious in the mind of jailers. To them, it was just what "junkies" go through.

While in jail, Larry Bell started showing symptoms related to his medical condition, addiction, that the DPD hadn't bothered finding out about when he came into the cell. He started spitting up blood and vomiting profusely. He hollered out vociferously that he was undergoing withdrawal, that he needed help. He was then being held in the DPD's male detention cell on the 9th floor — otherwise known then as the "torture chamber." As he cried out for help, the jailer, who was a supervisor, was told by a non-supervising officer about Larry's complaints. This officer described what he saw — the blood and vomiting. The response by the supervisor was (pardon this person's French here): "Fuck the dope fiend, let him die."

And they did. Larry was found dead in his cell the following day. A Board of Review, a process we have already described, was convened. Ultimately, no officer was held responsible for Larry's death. The autopsy called it a death of natural causes, not a homicide. The Board relied on the report of the medical examiner — a pattern that repeated with each and every jail death I describe here. We filed a lawsuit charging wrongful death, denial of medical treatment and denial of constitutional rights. The City of Detroit settled, paying six figures.

Poor Cheryl Brown's case was not much different. Cheryl was a drug addict, too, and was locked up in the 10th Precinct. She began complaining of withdrawal symptoms. The jailer reported this to her desk sergeant. The sergeant, who was female, refused to take any action. (I mention that the supervisor was female to illustrate that the attitude of indifference is gender-neutral.) The sergeant had a greater responsibility to get help than the jailer in Bell's case. So the jailer called EMS on her own, kudos to her. After EMS crew members arrived and checked Cheryl's vital signs, they offered to take Cheryl to the hospital. Incredibly, this sergeant refused to give them permission to do so.

The next day, Cheryl Brown was found dead in her cell. We sued the City of Detroit for denial of medical treatment. This case also settled for six figures. I will describe even worse cases, believe it or not. But first I must pause to decry that special brand of evil that permeates holding cells, jails and prisons. Once locked up, the misconduct jailers foist upon jail detainees illustrates even further how little humanity jailers saw in their detainees — and, ironically, how little they seemed to possess themselves. Think about it: There should be less rationale to harm a sick jail detainee who can't run, can't fight back, is always compliant, is no threat, is not resisting and to whom an undeniable duty to help is owed. Their only "crime" is a plea for help when they are ill.

But here, jail detainees cease to be human in an even more hopeless way than out on the street. In jail, the curtains are drawn and the only witnesses are members of the same staff, essentially potential co-conspirators. Other detainee witness accounts are presumed not credible by too many jailers. It's a matter of a "consider the source" kind of thinking. And yet, fellow jail detainees are your best witnesses for the simple reason that they've got nothing else to do. They're not distracted by other things. So the sounds are louder, the senses are more acute.

One highly respected expert witness we hired was Clinton L. Donaldson. He had vast experience as a police officer and commander; he also served as supervisor/investigator for the Internal Controls Division. He reviewed in his career literally thousands of police criminal misconduct cases and several "Prisoner Death" cases that were like Bell's. His conclusions were pretty damning. I quote just a few paragraphs from his deposition:

"I have reviewed and analyzed documents, written reports and evidence related to 'Prisoner Death' from case files assembled by the Detroit Police Department's Homicide Section. These official files demonstrate a consistent pattern whereby investigators collect information, write reports and omit important information that could have led to supervisors, police officers and detention officers being held accountable for the death of citizens who were in the custody of the Detroit Police Department.

"In the case files reviewed, no corrective action was taken against any

city employees, when the evidence clearly demonstrated a willful and reckless display of gross negligence by failing to follow the department's rules and regulations ...

"Homicide investigators failed to bring to the attention of the Chief of Police the extended period of illness that victim(s) encountered while being held in custody by the Detroit Police Department without proper medical attention, medication and mandatory constant observation ...

"In the case of Mr. Larry Bell (deceased), Homicide investigators never brought to the attention of the Chief of Police, Wayne County Medical Examiner or the Department's Internal Affairs Section the severe state of illness that Mr. Bell encountered while being incarcerated ..."

Donaldson described this illness: "... Regurgitating a blood-like substance for more than twenty-four hours and continually pleading for medical attention; lying on a dirty, unsanitary wooden bench and concrete floor for more than twenty-four hours in a fetal position, and continually pleading for medical attention; physically weakened from his deteriorating condition to the point that he could not stand in a show up," which most people know as a "lineup."

Donaldson reported that Larry was just shoved back into his cell with no medical attention. That no one in the department was held accountable for Larry's death, Donaldson said, illustrated a "lack of action on the part of the police department" which "demonstrates an ongoing problem in the police department as it relates to discipline of personnel who have the responsibility for maintaining custodial control over prisoners as noted in the Department's Rules and Regulations ..." He added that "a custom existed in the Detroit Police Department to fail to adequately, and objectively, investigate 'prisoner death' and to willfully and intentionally ignore and omit evidence which points to employee(s) culpability in prison death cases resulting in the department's inability to enforce their own policies, procedures and guidelines."

The DPD's "General Procedures" covered specific areas, including checking prisoners in cells every 30 minutes; use of detoxification/safety cells for people who are "chemically impaired," and that people in detox should be checked every 15 minutes; that all prisoners coming into the department's custody would be screened, and if they exhibited certain symptoms of alcohol or drug addiction, they should be placed into the detox cell *or*, I emphasize here, "transported to Detroit Receiving Hospital." Symptoms listed included "sweating, severe shaking or nausea/vomiting," among others. The procedures specifically required that "... prisoners, including those complaining of illness or wishing to take medication, shall be sent to Detroit Receiving Hospital (now DMC Detroit Receiving Hospital) as soon as possible."

Others in jail near or with Larry offered disturbing observations. One said Larry was too sick to sit on the bench in the waiting area for a lineup, and "he kept saying that he needed to go to the hospital because he was sick." This guy "heard (Larry) throwing up all night ... heard him call to the guard or trustee approximately four or five hours before anyone called for EMS. To his knowledge, the guards never responded to (Larry's) calls to them."

Another cellmate reported that while someone at the department was cleaning up the vomit in his cell, he heard Larry begin to "gag," and when asked, could not even make it to the toilet, and that Larry "kept calling for the officers and gagging." The cellmate "felt that the man was ... going to die."

The cases kept coming at me as I worked on the Bell and Brown suits. Sick prisoners, some even in dire need of emergency surgery, who asked for help were ignored and died pitiful deaths behind bars. As I contemplated all of this, I had what I call my "42 U.S.C. §1983 reckoning."

CHAPTER TWELVE

A Legal Reckoning

S o what the heck, you are asking, is 42 U.S.C. §1983?

Only what many consider to be the most important federal statute in contemporary American law, as one textbook puts it. This statute is derived from the Civil Rights Act of 1871. Its current, modern-day reading goes like this:

"*Every person who, under color of any statute, ordinance, regulation, custom or usage, of any State or Territory or the District of Columbia, subjects, or causes to be subjected any citizen of the United States or other person within the jurisdiction thereof to the deprivation of any rights, privileges or immunities secured by the Constitution and laws, shall be liable to the party injured in an action at law, suit in equity or other proper proceeding for redress. For the purposes of this section, any Act of Congress applicable exclusively to the District of Columbia shall be considered to be a state of the District of Columbia.*"

Some translation, according to the above-cited book, explains the wide reach of this statute:

Specifically, it "authorizes a court to grant relief when a party's federally protected rights have been violated by a state or local official or other person who acted under color of state law." In other words, if the official, city, county or state screws you over, you can turn to this statute for redress. And in fact, it has been used in the famous Supreme Court cases of *Brown v. Board of Education, Roe v. Wade, Reynolds v.*

Sims and *City of Richmond v. J.A. Croson Co.*

I will assume you are well familiar with the first two cases.

Reynolds v. Sims ruled that state legislature districts had to be roughly equal in population; in *City of Richmond v. J.A. Croson Co.*, the court held that the City of Richmond's minority set-aside program, which gave preference to minority business enterprises in the awarding of municipal contracts, was unconstitutional under the Equal Protection Clause.

As the textbook explains, this statute has been employed by many people alleging the use of excessive force, and is also used often by "public employees, prisoners, mental patients, recipients of public benefits, students, consumers, property owners and others who claim that state and local officials have violated their federal rights."

You can see why this statute is regarded as one of the most powerful tools for protection of people who are violated in any way by non-federal officials. These cases bring into sharpest relief my original motivation to become a lawyer so I could effect change. This was more like a reckoning. This was my opportunity to make the most important changes possible. Because unlike other areas of the law where mere compensation in cold cash was the reward, this was life and death itself. It was an intangible that resonated deeply within me. The kind of brutality, and even death, jail detainees so often endure at the hands of their jailers speaks of third-world dictatorships, of ancient ideas of humans as chattel. This wasn't supposed to happen here, and that it did, and so often, was like a punch in the gut. It made me nauseous.

I decided that this statute would be my weapon of choice, and a powerful one, in representing my clients, the unfortunate loved ones of those who had died in jail.

I also decided that I would cast a wider net, examining not just the cases I handled or knew of, but systematically analyzing the jail death culture, patterns, lack of accountability and ways I could help change all of this.

This was not a difficult decision. You cannot make up worse examples of deprivation of civil rights, not to mention heinous cruelty, than jail death cases. This had to stop.

I requested a list of jail deaths that had occurred in DPD's detention cell mausoleum. Among them were the likes of Mildred Brazil, a 70-something woman who had a heart condition, complained of chest pain, was not treated and died of a heart attack; Wayne Harris, who died of heat exhaustion; and Maude Patrick, a prostitute and $100-a-day heroin addict who complained repeatedly of stomach pain and vomiting. (She even had a seizure that was witnessed by one officer who did not further report it; another compassionate, dutiful officer reported these symptoms to the precinct desk there, including that Patrick asked to go to the hospital. This was denied, and Patrick died in jail.)

In Patrick's case, the precinct desk officer was found in neglect of duty, at least, for failing to follow this part of the Detroit Police Manual about "Prisoners Requiring Medical Attention":

"The officer in charge of the precinct desk shall investigate any cuts or bruises discernible on a prisoner which may be of recent origin ... Such prisoners, including those complaining of illness or wishing to take medication, shall be sent to Detroit Receiving Hospital as soon as possible ..."

There had been, in fact, 15 or 16 such victims at DPD over the previous 10 years — that's 1.5 jail deaths a year.

Each of these people complained of symptoms, were never properly monitored and died in misery and ignominy. Yeah, they were addicts, alleged criminals, maybe not society's best. But if you let them die, you are no better — and, I would argue, worse.

Even more tragically ironic, if any of these people had been standing right outside the police department's doors and shouted inside, "Officer, I'm having a heart attack," the officer would have called EMS or taken some other action.

There is technically no difference between those outside or inside detention cells. The Code of Ethics applies to all of them.

And yet, these cases were horrendous. How can you be so cruel?

Consider Tori Carter. She was a drug addict involved in a domestic dispute. She was arrested, but it was made known to police she had a drug problem. She was placed in an observation cell, the proper move at least. This meant she was no more than 25 feet from the door that led to the operations desk. In other words, she was well within hearing distance of officers and staff there.

She began crying for help; she was ignored by those who clearly heard her. Finally, her cellmate tried to call EMS on the phone inside the cell; she could not connect. The agony continued, and eventually, when Tori was unresponsive, officers called for help. It was too late. Tori died in that jail cell.

The DPD's evidence technicians took photos of many who were found dead in these cells. Here we encounter, thankfully, the stupidity so rife in these police departments again. They took photos of these bodies, lying on the floor in various ghoulish positions. (One guy died on the toilet; another was found dead on the cell bench.) What these photos showed me, via the frozen, bizarre postures many of them exhibited, was that rigor mortis had set in.

Conclusion: *They had not been checked every 30 or every 15 minutes. They hadn't been checked in hours.* Now, the police blotter read, "Checked every 30 minutes," but they either lied, or the "check" was a split-second "Yeah, he's still there."

My point: They are *looking at a dead person* every 30 minutes. But the blotter was used as evidence, i.e., cover-up.

The photos, the proof, was right in my hands.

In case I give you the impression these are confined to one, local police department, let me widen the lens with two grisly cases.

Abdul Akbar was a 59-year-old schizophrenic — a "red 6," in Wayne County, Mich., code — held in the county jail. He was there for "scrapping" — he stole metal to make his living. This doesn't hurt anyone, though it's illegal, and Akbar was a harmless guy. He was a father, brother, husband. He also had some mental illness issues, and his jailers were well aware of that. But he had no record of violence.

So he was arrested for scrapping in October 2014. He was in a pod, a holding area. He addressed the female guard because he had slept through breakfast, and also complained that a new medication he had gotten was making him feel uncomfortable.

The guard couldn't be bothered. She was watching movies and trying to find dates on the Plenty of Fish website on the county computer. She had an external hard drive she had obtained just for that purpose. On the job. It was later confirmed she was, in fact, watching movies during all of Akbar's pleas for help.

The officer wrote in her report that she told him she would see about getting him something to eat — presumably when her movie was over. She wrote that Akbar after a while "began to yell and make a strange noise as though he were in pain ... that Inmate Akbar leaned over her desk and grabbed the computer tower and monitor ... swinging them across the meal area."

She then said he climbed up and stood on the table, and looked like he was going to leap from it. That's when he collapsed.

Pause here. He *collapsed*. Already, it was obvious something medically was wrong with him, especially paired with what he had said about being in pain. But that seemed to escape attention.

Grabbing the computer is the only thing he could think of to get the guard's attention. Smart? No. But he never attacked her. Never touched her. Akbar then did in fact collapse on top of the table, according to most witness accounts.

Well, things got out of control quickly. The commotion woke up, literally, the other guard who was sleeping on duty that evening. This officer saw Akbar on top of the table with the computer — prior to his collapse. Out of panic, she told the movie-fan guard to call a Code 10, which means, "Officer needs help in the jail."

There is a policy among all officers. When you hear a Code 10, you drop everything and you all run to the officer's assistance. You do this as a "show of strength." So the first officers that arrived grabbed Akbar and slammed him to the floor. About 10 officers eventually were at the scene.

The movie fan-jailer later put up a post on Facebook about the "Righteousness of God," and that "Akbar got what he deserved." The sleeping guard posted on Facebook, "He was taken down so hard the building shook."

According to reports of other officers on the scene, Akbar would "not comply with ... instructions to stop his uncontrollable behavior." This is the "resisting arrest" cover. Code phrase, here, folks. There is a dispute about the extent to which, if at all, he was resisting arrest, but he had never been a threat to anyone. He had a history in the jail, so people knew that — knew that he was 59, just an old dude with a mental illness. One deputy testified he had interacted with Akbar and never knew of him to be anything other than quiet and introverted.

The woman then said that officers "successfully were able to gain control and secure Inmate Akbar in handcuffs."

But the main officer restraining Akbar wrote that he "administered a straight arm bar takedown placing Inmate Akbar on the floor." As we noted above, Akbar had already collapsed; some prisoners said he was unconscious. So where was the need to slam him to the ground?

The officer reported that once he got Akbar down, "everyone else began to try and help secure" him. Poor Akbar was outnumbered, and he "continued to make garbled noises."

This officer said Akbar was then handcuffed and taken through a door into a small, vestibule-like area that is closed off from other adjacent rooms. Uh-oh.

A number of other inmates later reported that while he was in this vestibule area, they heard Akbar, by then conscious again, screaming, yelling that he was being beaten and that he couldn't breathe.

The witnesses then heard only silence. Minutes later, Akbar was dragged to the elevator unconscious.

Akbar was taken to "segregation." This is where jailers take unruly inmates. Here, he was seen by a nurse, who later reported that he told her "he felt like his jaw had moved, and that he was sore." She said he was very "soft-spoken." Well, yeah. The nurse went through her routine. Later, during this investigation, she was asked for a log book report on this, and she said she would furnish it. That did not happen.

Several hours later, a video showed Akbar, by then barely conscious, "walking very slowly, and appearing to be having trouble standing upright or keeping his balance."

That day, Akbar also saw a mental health counselor who later reported that Akbar "refused to speak to her and appeared to be lethargic with no eye contact," and that "he nodded in agreement that he was being transferred to Division 1 for further evaluation."

Were these people blind? He is showing these symptoms and they basically goof around, taking their time, ignoring serious mental and physical symptoms — from the original incident on.

Sure enough, the Division 1 nurse reported Akbar "had a bump on his forehead and the left side of his jaw was swollen with a lump." Medical records also said Akbar told them, and they quoted it:

"I got stomped in my left jaw ... I got stomped in the face ... this morning and my left jaw is swollen and it's hard for me to open my mouth."

The conclusion we reached was that when he was in the vestibule, the deputies exacted their punishment on Akbar, on the mistaken belief that he had assaulted the female guard.

Hours later, Akbar finally was taken to Detroit Receiving Hospital. He told medical personnel he was assaulted and kicked in the head by officers in the jail. They found he had fractures on both sides of his jaw. They had to perform surgery.

A few days later, Akbar was discharged from the hospital and sent back to the jail. Four days later, he collapsed. After being delivered by EMS to the hospital again, he was pronounced dead.

Then came the investigation. The investigator ran into the solid "blue" wall. Akbar, investigators were told, initiated an "inmate assault" on the guard, though there was never any personal contact at all. There was no "assault" on the movie-fan jailer. Investigating this so-called "assault" on a movie-watching jailer, and her sleeping co-jailer, only reemphasizes the incestuous nature of "the code."

Now, there was plenty of "payback" from the officers who beat the crap out of Akbar, but no one was asking about that. The report notes that most of the 13 officers used identical wording to describe this, and that they refused to be interviewed. That left only the almighty "incident report," the eternal, etched-in-stone fantasy tale we analyzed earlier.

The big question was whether Akbar's death several days after the "inmate assault" was caused by the beating. The Wayne County Medical Examiner determined that the passage of time indicated he simply died of a heart attack. No one was charged for assault, obstruction of justice or misconduct by the Wayne County Prosecutor. The Prosecutor's Office issued a press release essentially waiving the autopsy report, stating there would be no charges, and that Akbar had a heart attack.

The Internal Affairs investigation implied that Akbar's jaw was fractured by the jailers, so his injuries were not self-inflicted. As Akbar himself said, "I got stomped in my left jaw." Thus, the obvious suspects were the officers who responded to that Code 10 and who beat Akbar in that vestibule area, right?

No sir. Every one of them denied anything other than using only the force necessary to contain the resisting Akbar. Nor did they see any other officer use excessive force. This is the cover-up. It's blue code. And it survives because we don't have video here — although there was video clearly showing an unconscious Akbar being dragged by officers into the elevator, and despite clear circumstantial evidence that Akbar was assaulted, and told people he was, and had the injuries, they still can lie and cover up. Akbar was denied treatment, beat up, died and no one was responsible.

I filed a civil lawsuit on behalf of Mr. Akbar — in search of another *Perry Mason* moment.

I know of many more cases. Unfortunately, defendants rely on legal arguments that prevent the public from learning the truth. Protective orders, which are routinely entered by courts, only serve defendants' interests, not those of plaintiffs, and protective orders are essentially ruses designed only to cover up the truth.

CHAPTER THIRTEEN

Claimed Justifications

T he video of the killing of Walter Scott couldn't have been more damning. Filmed by another of our conscientious civilians who happened to be nearby when Scott was running away from North Charleston, S.C., police officer Michael Slager, it is at once deeply disturbing — and irrefutable.

It shows Scott running away from Slager — as in the opposite direction, lest anyone try to mitigate this plain fact — and Slager pointing his gun and firing at Scott. Five bullets hit the target. Three hit Scott in the back, one in the buttocks and one on his ear.

No matter what anyone said later, you would assume the video would provide slam-dunk evidence that Slager basically murdered Scott, a 50-year-old black man who was a forklift operator. The video, which came out some time after the killing, also directly refuted Slager's police report. He not only had killed, he had lied. Pretty automatic case, right?

In fact, the jury in the criminal case against Slager could not reach a verdict.

How in the world did that happen?

Because it is nearly impossible to successfully prosecute in criminal courts police officers who have shot or killed civilians — in the line of duty, they claim. This is another major sinkhole in law enforcement.

I call this the claimed-justifications phenomenon.

Cops like Slager have at their disposal all kinds of ready-made justifications that arise out of the cop-as-hero culture. In fact, the justifications available to a police officer to avoid accountability in cases of deadly force, or any force, are limited only by the officer's imagination — at which point, his lawyer takes over and gives wings to those claimed justifications.

Among these justifications are some standbys that are most often used, and, unfortunately, are successful in deflecting justice against violent cops. These include:

"I feared for my life."

"I feared for my partner's life."

"He resisted arrest."

"I saw an object in his hand," or, as one defendant I knew put it, "I observed that he had a weapon up under his shirt, and I could see the outline of a large handgun."

"He would not comply."

"I only had a split second to make a decision."

"He was reaching down between the seats."

"He was coming toward me and he would not stop."

"He was much bigger and stronger than me."

"It was a high-crime area."

Cops have every right to defend themselves when justified. They are not paid to take a bullet. But when it comes to exercising ultimate force, we must find greater exactitude in evaluating the balance of constitutional protections and the self-interest of police officers trying to save their careers.

But as it stands now, it is abundantly easy for cops to deflect their misconduct through a multitude of potential hocus-pocus.

Let's take a closer look at the Scott-Slager case. This occurred April 4, 2015, and began with an altercation between the two men (both, ironically, had served in the U.S. Coast Guard). Slager, then 33 with five years as a police officer, stopped Scott because one of his car's brake lights was not working. Scott, his brother later said, was heading to the auto parts store to remedy that when Slager stopped him.

The scout car's dash cam shows Slager walking to Scott's car, talking to him and returning to the patrol car. At this point, Scott bolted out of his car and started running away.

Slager gave chase, caught up to Scott and they became entangled. Scott was able to break free and run again. Slager later reported that Scott managed to wrestle his Taser from him, which thus made Scott a threat. But Scott kept running. That's when Slager drew his gun and fired.

Now, let's hit the pause button and fill in some blanks, as reported by the media.

First, why did Scott take off during what should have been at most a minor violation? In the trial later, it was revealed that Scott knew that once Slager checked his license, he would learn a warrant had been issued for Scott's arrest for unpaid child support. Not smart, but not worth being shot to death.

Meanwhile, though Slager wrote in his police report that Scott managed to grab the Taser from him, he didn't know that a man named Feidin Santana was off in the distance. Santana saw Slager chasing Scott and the two men briefly struggling, with Slager "on top" of Scott, who was wriggling and trying to get away. Moments later, they both got up, with Scott fleeing. This part of the scene was not on the video, but was described by Santana later at trial.

So, in other words, Scott never took the Taser. But until the video surfaced showing the Taser fall to the ground at the scene of the scuffle, people believed Slager's report that he had. The video also showed Slager's partner, after Scott was shot, pick up something from the ground where Scott and Slager had wrestled, walk over to Scott's body and drop it there. Sound familiar?

Fast forward to Slager's testimony, and also his lawyer's comments, during the criminal trial. The evidence of the video notwithstanding, Slager pulled the excuses defense big time. At various times while testifying, he said:

"Scott would never stop after I gave him multiple commands to stop" (i.e., "He resisted arrest").

Scott was much stronger, so when he managed to grab Slager's Taser, "I knew I was in trouble … I was in total fear that Mr. Scott didn't stop, continued to come towards me" (i.e., "I feared for my life").

The prosecutor pointed out that even if Scott had had the Taser, the distance of about 18 feet between them would have rendered the Taser harmless. Slager responded, "At that time, I didn't have that information, so I can't answer that question" (i.e., "I had only a split second to make a decision," "He was coming toward me and wouldn't stop," etc.).

"So," the prosecutor asked, "would you agree that at this time, he is not armed and he's running away from you?"

Slager replied, "Like I said, at the time on April 4, I would say no, but after watching the video, yes." This remark has no category other than a pathetic repackaging of the "split-second" excuse, as was Slager's emotional remark that his mind was "like spaghetti" during this incident.

Scott was made out to be the aggressor in legal arguments. Defense attorneys said Scott's "… decision to attack a police officer" made Slager fear for his life and see little choice but to shoot Scott. The prosecutor responded to this concept, asking, "Should he have assumed that an unarmed man would have attacked a police officer?"

Nonetheless, the "feared for my life" excuse always has the potential of defying contrary physical evidence. The status afforded a cop by juries, judges and people in general must first be earned. But too often, the simple recitation of danger and fear confounds those in charge of keeping balance between cop and suspect.

Add to all of this that North Charleston was a predominantly black, lower-income area, while the police department was predominantly white. The department had received complaints of racial profiling and harassment, including excessive use of Tasers.

Despite all of this evidence and even Slager's admittance he was in error after the video was shown to all in court, the excuses managed to save him. The jury vote, true, was 11-to-1 to convict, but it was a hung jury nonetheless.

The conviction rate in criminal courts of cops like Slager is almost nonexistent. Civil court and out-of-court resolutions are far more common. North Charleston, for instance, paid Scott's family $6.5 million. Slager also faced federal charges for violating Scott's civil rights and for using a weapon unlawfully during the commission of a crime, among other charges. He took a plea deal and was sentenced to 20 years.

Again, the Scott/Slager case is not unusual. Cops literally get away with murder using the excuses, while also under the cover of heroism and a judicial system biased in favor of cops. We'll get to that in the next chapter.

Let's quickly look at the excuses used in some other cases. Several come from my own experience.

In 1998, Johnnie Crenshaw was shot by Jerold Blanding, a Detroit Police officer. Johnnie was making a withdrawal from an ATM at night. He was a 45-year-old learning-disabled factory worker. He had been driven by his friend to the ATM; while he was at the ATM, his friend moved her car to a different spot. When returning from the ATM, Johnnie mistakenly approached the wrong vehicle. It was late at night, and this vehicle was not unlike that of his friend. He had just his wallet and a credit card in his hand.

Unfortunately, this vehicle happened to belong to an off-duty cop, Jerold Blanding, who was with his girlfriend, also a cop, Tracey Elledge. She was at the vehicle's passenger door that Johnnie approached, thinking it was his friend's van.

The report said Elledge exclaimed, "Hey, what are you doing? Oh, shit." Johnnie immediately jumped back with his arms raised, realizing he was at the wrong vehicle. But before he or his friend, who was watching, could react, Blanding pulled his gun and opened fire. Johnnie was injured, but he got up and tried to run away. Blanding pursued him, shooting several more times. Johnnie survived, miraculously.

But it was a senseless shooting. Nonetheless, I quote from Blanding's report that seeks to "justify" this senseless shooting.

"Writer observed a black object in the subject's hand. Writer, fearing for Officer Elledge's life and my life, retrieved my dept. approved Glock 23 …

from under my shirt and fired 2 to 3 shots. The subject then ran ... into the parking lot heading towards Joy Road. Writer exited the vehicle and pursued the subject. The subject turned in writer's direction still holding the object in his hand. Writer, fearing for his life, fired a couple shots. Writer was 18 to 20 feet from the subject when shots were fired. The object fell to the ground and the subject took a couple of steps before falling to the ground. Writer approached the subject and identified myself as a police officer and ordered the subject not to move."

You will notice that along with the unnecessary shooting, it was only after Blanding shot, pursued and shot again that he said he was a police officer, and that he was 18 to 20 feet from Johnnie when shooting. A learning-disabled man, 18 to 20 feet distant — and running away from him. Such a threat.

In 2006, Harrick Beamon was beaten badly by three Detroit cops, James Markham, Kari Kammerzell and Sgt. Jason Sloan. Their story was that they saw Beamon walking away two times from a box truck parked in front of a club. They saw him reach behind him in his vehicle, out of their view. He was just looking for his keys — who hasn't done that on occasion?

But, as Markham wrote in his report, "With having knowledge of several (robberies) in the area, crew conducted an investigation on the same."

The officers approached Beamon in his car and "observed Beamon reaching around the interior of the vehicle." Next came the order for him to exit the car, Beamon's supposed refusal, profanity, his punching one of the officers and an ensuing fight, during which Beamon suffered serious injuries. Beamon did not have a gun, and no gun was found at the scene.

In a 2008 case I handled, Tommie Staples was shot and killed by Detroit Police Officers Barron Townsend and Steven Kopp. Staples was just walking down the street and happened to cross in front of the "semi-marked scout car," as the officers described it. The officers gave chase, killing Staples as he tried to run away. A weapon was later found at the scene, but there was no evidence linking it to Staples.

Kopp wrote, "... as he passed directly in front of us, I observed that he had his hand up under his shirt and I could see the outline of a large handgun ... As we were following him in the alley, the suspect stopped and pulled his weapon and pointed it at myself and my partner." Ordering him to stop, "he did not obey my commands and, fearing for my life, I fired 5 or 6 shots ..."

It's important to remember that this occurred at night, which raises the question: How did the cops discern the outline of the gun, given their distance from Staples and the darkness?

In the Lamar Grable/Officer Eugene Brown case, described in Chapters Seven through Nine, Brown testified that he saw a gun in Lamar's hand, and that Lamar was switching it from hand to hand, then tried to conceal it (i.e., "I saw an object in his hand").

In the case of Tamir Rice, the 12-year-old boy in Cleveland who was killed for having a toy gun, described in Chapter Three, a grand jury declined to indict Officers Timothy Loehmann, a rookie at the time, and his partner, Frank Garmback.

Here are some quotes reported by CNN and other media regarding that decision. As the prosecutor said, "Given this perfect storm of human error, mistakes and communications by all involved that day, the evidence did not indicate criminal conduct by police."

The prosecutor later stated that "it is likely that Tamir, whose size made him look much older and who had been warned his pellet gun might get him into trouble that day, either intended to hand it over to the officers or show them it wasn't a real gun. But there was no way for the officers to know that, because they saw the events rapidly unfolding in front of them from a very different perspective" (i.e., "I only had a split second to make a decision").

The prosecutor also referred to an FBI analysis of the video from that day, which showed Tamir "was drawing his gun from his waist" as the officers approached and got out of the scout car.

Other excuses are that the officers never got the information that Tamir was a juvenile and the gun was probably not real (but which, as we discussed, still did not call for killing the boy); and that officers showed up ready to face a "possible active shooter in a neighborhood with a history of violence" (i.e., "It's a high-crime area").

Two officers had been killed there, in fact, he said, adding, "Police are trained that it only takes a third of a second or less to draw and fire a weapon at them. Therefore, they must react quickly to any threat." We know the name of this excuse.

A Cleveland judge later reviewed the case and found probable cause for a number of charges against Loehmann, including involuntary manslaughter, reckless homicide, negligent homicide and dereliction of duty. Garmback was charged with negligent homicide and dereliction of duty. The judge rejected aggravated murder charges against both officers.

Due to various legal complications too laborious to describe here, the officers could not actually be arrested. The case was unresolved as of this writing.

The "bogeyman" excuse is one often used, as we saw in the case of Michael Brown and Darren Wilson that garnered national headlines. Officer Wilson used that among other excuses in his grand jury testimony.

Wilson said Brown was as big as a "demon," a "monster," with tremendous strength. "When I grabbed him, the only way I can describe it is I felt like a 5-year-old holding onto Hulk Hogan."

Wilson characterized Brown as aggressive and combative. Brown's friends contradicted, but it's easy to indict the character of a dead man. Wilson also compared Brown to a Balrog, a J.R.R. Tolkien fictional creature, and that a punch from Brown "in my face could knock me out or worse … I've already taken two to the face … the third one could be fatal if he hit me right."

Other descriptions of Brown, a *Slate* magazine reporter wrote, "sits flush with a century of stereotypes" used to justify violence against African Americans. The same technique was used by George Zimmerman when describing Trayvon Martin. Wilson kept piling on this kind of description, and the fear-for-my-life against a big-black-bogeyman. These excuses worked; the grand jury did not indict Wilson.

On it goes. In 2014 in Chicago, Officer Jason Van Dyke fired 16 shots at Laquan McDonald, an African American who was just 17 years old. According to *The New York Times* and other media reports, police responded to a call that McDonald was breaking into vehicles and carrying a knife. When police arrived, they reported he used the knife to slice a patrol car tire, and walked away from repeated orders by police to drop the knife.

A video of the shooting showed later that it was Van Dyke who went after McDonald while McDonald was walking away. The video shows clearly that McDonald was a good distance from the police vehicle, yet his body took the hit and collapsed in the street as Van Dyke shot him anyway.

After McDonald lay on the ground, Van Dyke fired more — 16 times in all, in about 15 seconds. Reportedly, Van Dyke was on the scene for under 30 seconds before firing, and just six seconds after exiting his car.

Six seconds. The first officer on the scene was said to have seen no need to use deadly force, and several other officers on the scene did not fire their weapons, either. McDonald died a short time after being taken to the hospital.

McDonald had been a deeply troubled youth with mental health issues of various kinds. He had been in plenty of trouble with drugs. So he was not likeable or admirable. But he was not doing anything at that time to warrant being shot even once, not to mention 16 times.

Van Dyke and seven other officers were recommended to be fired for making or backing up the fictional version of this senseless killing. The seven others were accused of filing false police reports, so that blue code worked well for Van Dyke, even from officers who had not used deadly force against McDonald. They reported that McDonald had moved "menacingly" toward Van Dyke with his knife. That the video showed otherwise, again, seemed not to register to Van Dyke.

Still Van Dyke pleaded not guilty, using the feared-for-my-life excuse. He was suspended without pay pending trial. Meanwhile, protests were held and various reforms were suggested or carried out. McDonald's family was awarded a $5 million settlement from the Chicago City Council.

In another case, in Minnesota, Officer Jeronimo Yanez was charged with second-degree manslaughter and two felony counts of dangerous discharge of a firearm after shooting to death Philando Castile in July 2016. Yanez pulled Castile over because he thought Castile and his fiancée, Diamond Reynolds, resembled suspects in a convenience store robbery that had occurred a few days prior. (Reynolds' 4-year-old daughter was also in the car, unfortunately.) The vehicle had a non-working taillight as well.

Yanez approached Castile, who was respectful and compliant. He first gave Yanez his insurance card and then informed Castile he had a firearm and a permit to carry it. This is what you are legally required to do — and Castile did so. Yanez suddenly just freaked out and told Castile not to reach for his gun. Castile responded, twice, that he wasn't doing that.

Castile was just reaching for his wallet, but Yanez didn't wait for that. He pulled his gun and rapidly fired seven times.

Reynolds, who must have been in near shock, had the presence of mind to start live streaming onto Facebook the bloody scene about 40 seconds after the final shot. Castile uttered, as he died, "I wasn't reaching for it."

Castile's gun was in his pocket, but there wasn't even a bullet in the chamber. And he clearly was not reaching for it.

Yanez fell back on several justifications. He was quoted as saying that Castile was reaching down between his right leg and center console of the car at the same time he said he had a gun. "And he put his hand around something," with his hand forming a "C-shape," as if to grasp the butt of a gun.

After Castile's hand disappeared from Yanez's view, he said, "I know he had an object and it was dark. And he was pulling it out with his right hand, and as he was pulling it out, a million things started going through my head. And I thought I was going to die."

Since he thought Castile had the gun, he had "no option" other than to pull his gun and shoot.

So here we have the "He was reaching down between the seats"; "I saw an object in his hand"; "I had only a split second to make a decision"; and "I feared for my life" standard justifications. Plus he threw in the "spaghetti" head for good measure.

Yanez was put on administrative leave pending trial. In November 2016, he entered no plea. He was later acquitted.

These excuses are at grave variance with what the law requires, because while a police officer can legitimately use deadly force if there is a threat of harm, the harm has to meet certain criteria.

Specifically, that harm must be significant, imminent and reasonable. These words are often omitted when officers put forth their grandiose excuses. For instance, in the case of Abdul Akbar, described in Chapter Twelve, he is swinging the computer tower — but he's 10 to 15 feet away, and if he's that far away, this is not a threat that is significant, imminent or reasonable. It's more accurate to say Akbar was attacking the computer than the jailer.

In the Walter Scott case, if Scott is running away from Slager, where is the imminent threat? When he says basically that he didn't know if Scott had a gun and that he feared Scott might suddenly turn around and shoot him — this is not an *imminent threat*. This is a *what-if.* You can't kill somebody for what-ifs.

But cops are getting away with telling what-ifs in ways that make juries see imminent threat. Cops, and their defense lawyers, have this down to a science. They tap into the fear factor and focus on everything the victim did wrong — not what the cop did. Fear always overshadows common sense, and that lets defense lawyers get away with Houdini tactics.

So it is that successful prosecutions of cops who harm or kill civilians are rare. Only awareness and exposure of the abuse of these excuses and of the "imminent threat" defense will help reduce such tragedies. And, as with the other suggestions in this book, it would not only be good for civilians, it would help cops, too.

CHAPTER FOURTEEN

The More Things Change...

Remember Rodney King?

Most anyone over 35 does. We wince when we remember the video — and what a quaint, old-fashioned videotape it was compared to today's clean, digital cell phone images. It showed several white cops surrounding King, who was black, and taking turns beating him while other cops watched.

It was March 3, 1991, in Los Angeles. The cops and King had been involved in a high-speed car chase, according to various media reports. Two others, Bryant Allen and Freddie Helms, were in the car with King. They all earlier had been watching football and drinking. When California Highway Patrol officers noticed King's speeding car, they pursued him. King refused to pull over and just went faster. He later explained that he tried to evade police because he knew a DUI would violate his parole for a robbery conviction.

Yes, like many other victims of police brutality, King was far from a model citizen. He even had pleaded "no contest" to battery after beating his wife. He also had threatened the store owner with an iron bar when he committed the robbery.

He was in his mid-20s the day of the car chase. As it dragged on, several L.A. police cars and a police helicopter become involved. This posse finally managed to corner King's car. Then things got ugly.

Allen and Helms both were beaten after exiting the car. When King finally got out, he was gagged and patted down. Before long, King was surrounded by LAPD cops, who had taken over the scene from the Highway Patrol officers. In charge was Sgt. Stacey Koon. The others were Laurence Powell, Timothy Wind, Theodore Briseno and Rolando Solano.

It was at this point that a man named George Holliday began videotaping what was going on from his apartment nearby. King had already been Tasered twice. As described by Wikipedia, the videotape begins at the point King is lying on the ground.

Then, the tape shows, "he rises and rushes toward Powell — as argued (later) in court, either to attack Powell or to flee — but regardless King and Powell both collided in the rush ... Officer Powell strikes King with his baton, and King is knocked to the ground. Powell strikes King several more times with his baton. Briseno moves in, attempting to stop Powell from striking again, and Powell stands back. Koon reportedly said, 'That's enough.'"

King then rose to his knees. Powell and Wind began again hitting him with their batons. Koon ordered them to use "power strokes."

Then "... King continues to try to stand again. Koon orders the officers to 'hit his joints, hit the wrists, hit his elbows, hit his knees, hit his ankles.'" King sustained 33 strikes and six kicks. He was handcuffed and his legs were restrained as well, and he was dragged on his stomach to the side of the road until an ambulance could arrive.

King survived but sustained multiple, serious injuries, including skull fractures, brain damage, broken bones, kidney failure and emotional trauma. He sued the City of Los Angeles and won $3.8 million, and $1.7 million in attorney fees.

The four LAPD cops were charged with assault with a deadly weapon and use of excessive force. All were initially either acquitted or let off the hook via a hung jury. Federal charges later led to two of the four being found guilty of violating King's civil rights.

Prior to this, Holliday had offered to show the LAPD his videotape, but they refused, for whatever reason. So he took it to KTLA television, which later broadcast those images we all still remember.

This was one of the first times a private citizen recorded such an incident — and it went viral. It was broadcast all over the world, the first such wide exposure of this kind of evidence.

So here we are, nearly 30 years later — and when it comes to cop-citizen confrontation, and the subsequent fates of the offending cops, what has changed?

Very little, as we have demonstrated in this book. Despite the seemingly ever-present cell phone-armed citizens recording so many of these incidents, charges either are never filed, or juries acquit or cannot reach decisions.

In determining why so little has changed, there is more at work here than the ongoing cop-can-do-no-wrong syndrome we have discussed at length.

A great deal more.

This has to do with the courts, and the judiciary. It has to do with judicial appointments and how opinions often reflect more than just the facts in a case.

Judges in this country are supposed to be nonpartisan, according to the law. The goal of this is impartiality — or at least, the appearance of it. In reality, this supposed impartiality is what is called a "legal fiction." Judges may be conservative or liberal, and their bent emerges in the decisions they write.

Federal court judges are appointed by U.S. presidents for life. So a conservative president will nominate a judge he believes will decide issues along his or her political party's way. While generally judges in state courts run for election, where there is a vacancy, the Governor may appoint a judge to fill that vacancy. The same principle of potential bias applies. Thus, a majority opinion written by a conservative or liberal judge can be crafted to fashion a desired outcome.

With this in mind, it's important to become familiar with four long-standing Supreme Court decisions that have shaped the course of protections and immunities for police. In all, the decisions were based on facts generated by the cop on the beat.

While only these few cases meandered their way to the Supreme Court, the impact was seminal. "Seminal" cases create precedents that others are bound to follow, thus they remain on the books, are cited frequently and form the basis for decisions that impact lives well into the future.

In some cases, this leads to judge-created language that becomes part of a beat cop's arsenal of words. One example is the phrase "split-second decision," an often relied-upon justification for the use of excessive force which you have read in this book often. Another court decision mentions "hazy borders," implying there are gray areas in certain factual situations where holding a cop's feet to the fire is considered too harsh an outcome.

So what guilty cops got away with before recordings proved them wrong, they still too often get away with. The recordings have not changed the game when it comes to prosecuting guilty cops.

Here is a brief summary of these four U.S. Supreme Court opinions that continue to govern judicial outcomes in cases involving police use of excessive force:

Graham v. Connor: This was a 1989 case where the Court outlined what constitutes a "reasonable standard" when a citizen claims a police officer used excessive force. This decision legitimizes the "split-second decision" justification, without benefit of hindsight offered by today's video evidence. "Split-second decision" shows a court creating language that becomes a utility for police misconduct.

Saucier v. Katz: In this 2001 ruling, the Court defined the level of "qualified immunity" of federal police officers who face lawsuits by citizens in federal court. This case especially examined what the opinion called the "hazy border between excessive and acceptable force."

Brosseau v. Haugen: This December 2004 case dealt with whether a police officer who shot a suspect in the back as he was trying to get away in his car was entitled to qualified immunity. The circuit court held the officer was not entitled to immunity. Notably, however, the Supreme Court opinion, while not upsetting the appellate court's opinion, left the question open and suggested Brosseau's actions fell in the "hazy border between excessive and acceptable force." This creative language leans in a conservative direction, which fosters more excuses for officers to avoid accountability.

Tennessee v. Garner: This 1985 case tested a Tennessee statute that "provides that if, after a police officer has given notice of an intent to arrest a criminal suspect, the suspect flees or forcibly resists, the officer may use all the necessary means to effect the arrest," as described on *caselaw.findlaw.com.* A man suspected of burglary was killed by a police officer even though the man was fleeing and not armed. The Court found this law to be unconstitutional, a good opinion. The seminal impact of *Tennessee v. Garner* implied a stricter standard, in a sense, to judge when an officer can use deadly force. It required that not a general threat be posed but that a significant threat of death or serious physical injury be posed to an officer or others. This was a good decision. However, in recent years under more conservative courts, this seeming level of scrutiny has become more cop-preferential.

So now, we have seen facts in official police reports clearly controverted by independent digital evidence captured by citizen surveillance. We've seen this divergence in many of these recent cases, including those mentioned in this volume:

Rodney King
Michael Brown
Eric Garner
Corey and Trammel Proctor, and Jeremy Smith
The woman on the bus in L.A.
Arthur Chapman
Abdul Akbar
Walter Scott
Philando Castile
Tamir Rice
Laquan McDonald
Harrick Beamon
Tommie Staples

These and other recent cases raise the question: What should judges do, in the absence of digital disputed evidence, with a set of facts based only on the officer's word, and in the absence of any refutation by a dead victim?

Legitimate seeds of doubt now planted by independent digital evidence need judicial cultivation. No one disagrees cops need protection and immunity. But a clear lie cannot serve as the basis to create a standard. It would be a false standard. Our citizens, the victims we have profiled in this book, deserve much more.

In cases today that have no disputed digital evidence, what level of scrutiny should at least be considered in judging an officer's claims of justification? In legal parlance, leave it to the jury as a question of fact. But as it stands now, when there is no recording, we start at square one: Defer to the cop's word. This means that without contrary evidence, a cop can just plant a gun, say what happened and no one questions him.

Let's look at all of this with a new lens.

It is time to draw a distinction between what is considered credible evidence today versus back before this evidence existed — conditions three of the four Supreme Court cases largely reflected. It is time to offset with new considerations the current conservative thought process that still rests on the seminal cases, which created this body of language that shields officers at any given point.

What is all the more frustrating is the contrast in these cases between criminal and civil court outcomes. The four seminal cases made it to the Supreme Court because a question of law in each of them had to be resolved or clearly stated.

The glaring irony is that outside of this criminal court corral, the victims or their surviving families so often are granted huge settlements in civil court or awarded huge out-of-court settlements by police departments. What does that say about the criminal case that lets cops off the hook?

Simply put, in cases where such evidence does not exist, there should be some recognition, some kind of allowance of what we now know about independent digital evidence. There should be more room for doubt in the stories told by all police officers when it comes to the ultimate exercise of force.

There should be acknowledgment that we are now in the era of independent digital, citizen-gathered evidence, and that this kind of evidence will only become more common. Until we give due recognition to this era inside our courtrooms, each grisly scene where cops exercise power, not authority, can with impunity destroy the lives of innocent citizens.

This cannot stand.

CLOSING ARGUMENTS

I hope that, if nothing else, I have made clear in this book that policing requires unique, human skill. While it generally takes only 16 to 20 weeks of training, the demands of the job might well require the equivalent of a Ph.D. — at least, in Human Interaction.

The reflections offered in this book have given dimension to what society demands from those it wishes to append the status of hero — and why these demands exist.

Human propensity underpins all conduct. Hero status must be earned at all times, and displayed at all times — in danger, in temptation, in interpersonal strife and in calm. This cannot be too much to ask of people entrusted with the ultimate authority to do what no one else on Earth can do: Take a life. It is as simple as it is complex: Behind every good cop is a healthy conscience.

A doctor has in his hands the responsibility of life and death. There is no amount of stress that excuses his negligent use of a scalpel. A police officer has at his disposal dozens of excuses to color his human professional interactions with citizens.

Where those excuses are used deceptively to justify those interactions, a true betrayal exists. The covenant to "protect and serve" should not ring hollow. A good job today does not excuse bad behavior tomorrow.

The observations in this book exploring how humanness defines character are the very things that escape the mindset of most police officers who serve the public. Such observations remain rare in the public square and in public discourse, as presented in Chapter Fourteen.

But there are a few rays of hope that, with the proliferation of cell phone-bearing citizens, there may come a tipping point where cops no longer can assume the cover they've enjoyed so far.

A major *BuzzFeed News* investigation in 2016 examined the issues I have raised. This 7,000-word exhaustive article, written by Albert Samaha, came to many of the same conclusions presented in this book: that cops lie for a variety of reasons; that the most common cover for cops accused of perjury is "inventing probable cause after an arrest"; that cops "take sides" in court, though they aren't supposed to; and much more.

But the article also noted a growing awareness by cops and police departments that the game is changing, due to the skyrocketing number of citizen-recorded cell phone videos. One police official calls this "a new era for us."

Another new book also addresses police shootings. *Blue on Blue: An Insider's Story of Good Cops Catching Bad Cops* by Charles Campisi, former NYPD Chief of Internal Affairs Bureau, documents a reduction in the number of fatal shootings of citizens by police in New York City and nationally, among other issues. While I am cautious about undue optimism, I am glad to see scrutiny of any kind.

I add my voice to these, hoping the momentum builds. My own personal insights as an African American born in a segregated world, a former police officer, a police department attorney and a crusader against police intransigence offers unique perspective and — I hope — solutions for police misconduct and misuse of authority.

As a human being who has walked in police boots, I repeat again my first commandment in the march forward to a better police culture: Police officers are human beings first, and heroes only when they remember that.

ABOUT THE AUTHOR

David A. Robinson, Esq., operates his law firm, Robinson & Associates Inc., in the Detroit suburb of Southfield. Specializing in police misconduct litigation, Robinson has handled hundreds of matters involving wrongful arrests and wrongful deaths at the hands of police officers during his 33-year career as an attorney. He has obtained million dollar-plus settlements and verdicts in non-lethal police chase, accident and shooting cases. Robinson has also successfully litigated several cases involving deaths of pretrial detainees in Detroit jails.

Early in his adult life, Robinson worked for the Detroit Police Department (DPD), both as an officer and as an attorney. During his time with the DPD, he defended officers in civil litigation matters and taught the legal section of recruit training at the Detroit Metropolitan Police Academy. He also held a teaching position with the Wayne State University Criminal Justice Department.

Robinson sits on the executive board of the Legal Redress Committee for the NAACP. He is a former member of the Michigan Association of Justice (MAJ) and the National Lawyers Guild (NLG). Previously, he served on the MAJ and NLG executive boards. He has also lectured on police misconduct at seminars sponsored by Lorman Education Services, Professional Education Systems Institute, MAJ, NLG and National Police Accountability Project. A 1979 graduate of Wayne State University, Robinson received his Juris Doctor degree from Detroit College of Law in 1985.